OECD ECONOMIC SURVEYS

1993-1994

DENMARK

ORGANISATION FOR ECONOMIC CO-OPERATION AND DEVELOPMENT

ORGANISATION FOR ECONOMIC CO-OPERATION AND DEVELOPMENT

Pursuant to Article 1 of the Convention signed in Paris on 14th December 1960, and which came into force on 30th September 1961, the Organisation for Economic Co-operation and Development (OECD) shall promote policies designed:

- to achieve the highest sustainable economic growth and employment and a rising standard of living in Member countries, while maintaining financial stability, and thus to contribute to the development of the world economy;
- to contribute to sound economic expansion in Member as well as non-member countries in the process of economic development; and
- to contribute to the expansion of world trade on a multilateral, non-discriminatory basis in accordance with international obligations.

The original Member countries of the OECD are Austria, Belgium, Canada, Denmark, France, Germany, Greece, Iceland, Ireland, Italy, Luxembourg, the Netherlands, Norway, Portugal, Spain, Sweden, Switzerland, Turkey, the United Kingdom and the United States. The following countries became Members subsequently through accession at the dates indicated hereafter: Japan (28th April 1964), Finland (28th January 1969), Australia (7th June 1971), New Zealand (29th May 1973) and Mexico (18th May 1994). The Commission of the European Communities takes part in the work of the OECD (Article 13 of the OECD Convention).

3 2280 00497 9779

Publié également en français.

Table of contents

Tables

Diagrams

BASIC STATISTICS OF THE DENMARK

THE LAND

Area (1 000 sq. km)	43	Inhabitants in major cities, 1.1.1993,	
Agricultural area (1 000 sq. km), 1988	28	thousands:	
		Copenhagen	466
		Aarhus	271
		Odense	181
		Aalborg	157

THE PEOPLE

Population, 1.1.1994, thousands	5 197	Civilian employment, 1991,	
Number of inhabitants per sq. km	121	thousands	2 647
Net natural increase average (1990-1993, thousands)	5	By sector:	
Net natural increase per 1 000 inhabitants,1993	0.1	Agriculture	149
		Industry	557
		Construction	167
		Market services	924
		Government	850

PRODUCTION

Gross domestic product, 1993		Gross fixed capital formation in 1993	
(Kr million)	876 856	(Kr million):	129 835
GDP per head (1993 US$)	26 030	Per cent of GDP	14.8
		Per head (US$)	3 854

THE GOVERNMENT

Public consumption, in 1993		Composition of Parliament (no. of seats):	
(percentage of GDP)	26	Social Democrats	69
General government current revenue in 1992		Conservatives	30
(percentage of GDP)	57	People's Socialists	15
Public gross fixed capital investment in 1992		Liberals	29
(percentage of GDP)	2	Progressive Party	12
		Social Liberalists	7
		Center Democrats	8
		Christian Democrats	4
		Greenland and Faroe Islands	4
		Independant	1
		Total	179
Last general elections: 12.12.1990		Next general elections: 11.12.1994 at the latest	

FOREIGN TRADE

Exports of goods and services as		Imports of goods and services as	
percentage of GDP, 1993	35	percentage of GDP, 1993	27
Main exports in 1992, percentage of		Main imports in 1992, percentage of	
total merchandise exports,		total merchandise imports:	
Agricultural products	14	Intermediate goods for agriculture	4
Canned meat and canned milk	2	Intermediate goods for other sectors	45
Industrial goods	70	Fuels and lubricants	6
Other goods	14	Capital goods	11
		Transport equipment	5
		Consumer goods	26

THE CURRENCY

Monetary unit: Krone		Currency units per US$,	
		average of daily figures:	
		Year 1993	6.482
		April 1994	6.659

Note: An international comparison of certain basic statistics is given in an annex table.

This Survey is based on the Secretariat's study prepared for the annual review of Denmark by the Economic and Development Review Committee on 25 May 1994.

•

After revisions in the light of discussions during the review, final approval of the Survey for publication was given by the Committee on 24 June 1994.

•

The previous Survey of Denmark was issued in February 1993.

Introduction

Economic growth resumed in the second half of 1993, despite the recession in Denmark's major trading partners. In contrast to the 1987-92 period, demand expansion is being domestically generated. Monetary stability, underpinned by ERM membership, has been successful in creating the conditions for recovery, inflation being low and interest rates having come down. The current account is in surplus and the debt problems of the private sector have been substantially corrected. The budgetary consolidation of the late 1980s put the public finances on a relatively sound footing and provided the platform for some temporary fiscal support for demand. With both the monetary and fiscal stance set to ease further in 1994, economic growth is likely to exceed potential rates this year and next, allowing employment to expand for the first time since 1987.

Unemployment is, nevertheless, set to remain high and remains the most serious economic problem. The causes are rather complex and relate substantially to labour-market rigidities. There is, however, a recognition that the wealth- and employment-creating capacity of the economy depends on the business-sector environment and this has prompted a re-examination of government policies towards business. Public policy in Denmark has a long tradition of non-intervention, with resource allocation mostly left to market forces. While the advantages associated with this approach are widely recognised, the view has gained ground that the government could play a more active role in improving the business environment. Policy has accordingly shifted towards the encouragement of stronger links between government and business.

Part I of the Survey reviews economic developments since Denmark was previously examined by the EDRC, highlighting the recovery in activity in the course of 1993. Part II discusses the evolution of monetary and budgetary policies during this period, against the background of currency-market turbulence and the use of fiscal policy to support demand and employment. Recent measures to reduce structural unemployment are also reviewed and assessed. Part III presents short-run projections and discusses risks. The special chapter of the Survey (Part IV) examines the re-orientation of policies towards the business sector in light of past performance and recent policy initiatives. Conclusions are given in Part V.

I. Recent Trends

The Danish recession appears to have been more abrupt and shorter than in neighbouring countries (Table 1). Having been through a period of protracted weakness in domestic demand since 1987, during which support for activity was

Table 1. **Economic performance indicators: international comparison**

	1991	1992	1993	1992	1993	
				II	I	II
GDP growth rate (s.a.a.r.)						
Denmark	**1.0**	**1.2**	**1.2**	**−2.1**	**0.8**	**5.2**
OECD Europe	2.6	1.1	−0.2	−0.6	−0.8	1.5
EC	3.2	1.0	−0.4	−0.8	−0.9	1.3
OECD	1.4	1.7	1.2	1.2	0.9	2.1
Total domestic demand (s.a.a.r.)						
Denmark	**−0.5**	**−0.7**	**0.4**	**−4.7**	**1.6**	**3.2**
OECD Europe	3.7	1.2	−1.2	−0.3	−2.5	0.8
EC	4.4	1.2	−1.7	−0.5	−3.3	0.5
OECD	1.3	1.7	1.1	1.3	0.6	2.1
Unemployment rate						
Denmark	**10.5**	**11.2**	**12.2**	**11.3**	**12.2**	**12.3**
OECD Europe	8.6	9.6	10.7	9.9	10.3	11.1
EC	9.2	10.3	11.3	10.6	11.0	11.6
OECD	7.1	7.8	8.2	8.0	8.1	8.3
Consumer price inflation (a.r.)						
Denmark	**2.2**	**2.1**	**1.7**	**2.0**	**1.6**	**1.8**
OECD Europe minus Turkey	5.3	4.4	3.8	3.5	4.2	3.3
EC	5.2	4.5	3.8	3.5	4.2	3.3
OECD	5.1	4.2	3.5	3.6	4.0	2.5

Source: OECD.

Diagram 1. KEY FEATURES OF ECONOMIC ACTIVITY

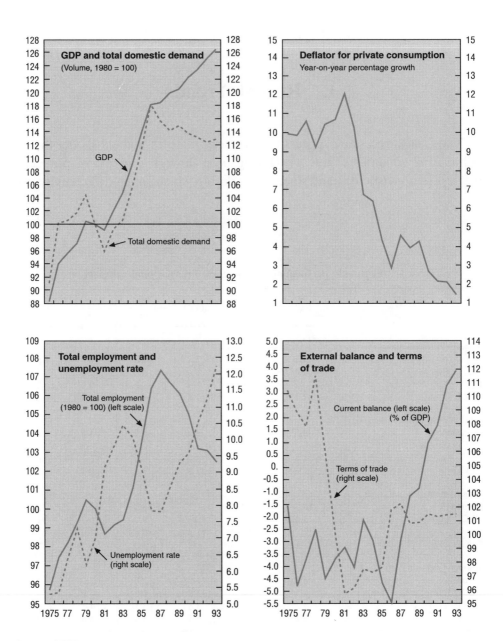

Source: OECD.

Diagram 2. **THE DANISH ECONOMY: A SNAPSHOT**

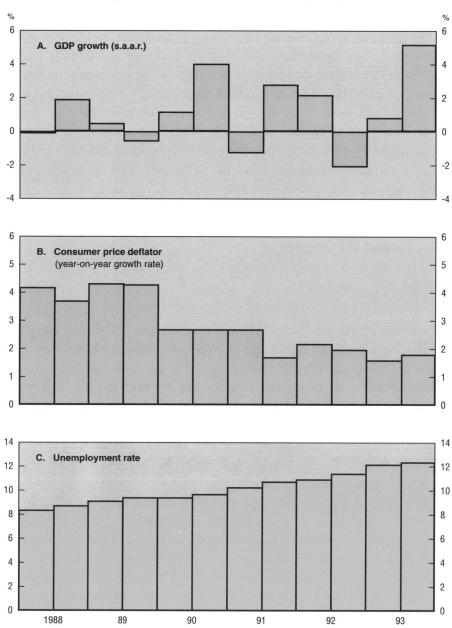

Source: OECD.

provided mainly by strong export demand, GDP declined in the second half of 1992 (Diagrams 1 and 2). However, instead of deepening with the international recession, domestic demand underwent a long-awaited pick-up in 1993. A tentative recovery could already be detected in the first half of the year, when the impulse from external demand was still waning, and output expansion has since been more vigorous than in most neighbouring countries. Employment nevertheless evolved much in line with the rest of Europe, falling for the sixth consecutive year. The resulting increase in unemployment contributed to further consolidation of gains on the inflation front, price inflation being significantly lower than the OECD average. On the other hand, the strengthening of the external balance was more modest than in preceding years.

Factors behind the recovery

Domestic demand

The retrenchment of domestic demand in the late 1980s and early 1990s reflected hesitant spending on the part of both households and businesses. Private consumption fell in the closing years of the 1980s and, despite some recovery, household spending on goods and services had not regained its 1986 level by 1992. Indeed, sluggish demand and spare capacity kept business capital spending on a downward trend, with uncertainty over the Maastricht Treaty an additional depressing factor in 1992. The only major domestic demand component to register increases during the 1987-1992 period was public consumption.

This protracted weakness in domestic demand gave way to recovery in 1993. The pick-up reflected a steepening increase in total consumption and a slower rate of decline in total fixed investment (Table 2). More expansionary fiscal policy (see below) showed up in strong advances in public consumption and there was also a robust increase in the growth of private consumption, a rate of growth of 7.5 per cent (s.a.a.r.) being recorded in the second half of the year. However, the decline in both residential and business construction continued to depress demand. Machinery investment was broadly stable in 1993 due to a strong increase in the second half of the year, while substantial destocking reduced total domestic demand.

14

Table 2. **Domestic demand developments**

Percentage year-on-year change, 1980 prices

	1989	1990	1991	1992	1993	1993	
						I	II
Private consumption	−0.4	0.0	1.4	0.7	2.6	0.9	4.2
Goods	−1.2	0.1	3.2	0.4	1.5	−0.9	3.8
Non-durables	−1.2	−0.3	2.8	2.0	2.1	1.3	2.8
Semi-durables	−0.7	0.2	4.4	−2.6	2.5	2.9	2.1
Durables, excluding autos	2.2	1.0	2.6	−1.7	3.5	−0.8	7.6
Automobiles	−8.7	1.7	3.7	0.4	−11.2	−28.1	17.5
Services	1.7	0.2	0.8	0.7	3.9	3.3	4.5
Investment	1.0	−1.7	−5.4	−8.2	−1.8	−4.4	0.9
Residential construction	−8.9	−13.7	−11.8	−4.1	−3.1	−6.6	0.2
Business construction	−13.1	−3.4	−10.9	−4.0	−11.7	−7.8	−15.0
Civil engineering	8.8	3.1	−16.3	10.4	−4.7	4.6	−13.2
Transportation equipment	32.6	−1.2	25.6	−31.8	16.6	14.3	19.6
Machinery	5.1	2.7	−2.6	−10.2	−0.6	−10.8	10.9
Government consumption	−0.6	−0.4	0.0	0.7	3.2	3.1	3.3
Final domestic demand	−0.2	−0.4	−0.3	−0.9	2.0	0.7	3.4
Stockbuilding [1]	0.7	−0.6	−0.2	0.2	−1.5	−2.1	−1.0
Total domestic demand	0.5	−1.0	−0.5	−0.7	0.4	−1.6	2.3

1. Contribution to GDP growth.
Source: Danmarks Statistik, *Nationalregnskaber.*

The quickening pace of private consumption growth reflected gains in real incomes, the household saving ratio undergoing a modest rise in 1993 (Diagram 3). In spite of falling employment, households' real disposable income continued to increase, benefiting both from an expansion in government transfers and real wage increases. The failure of real income gains to be fully reflected in spending increases can partly be ascribed to greater uncertainty: consumer sentiment indicators collapsed in the last quarter of 1992 and remained depressed in the first half of 1993 (Diagram 4). The reluctance to increase spending may also have reflected the continued need to consolidate household finances (see Part III), together with the lagged effects of earlier declines in house prices. Private saving appears to be rather sensitive to the value of household assets, including the housing stock.[1]

15

Diagram 3. **THE PRIVATE SECTOR: SAVING AND NET LENDING**

(as a per cent of disposable income)

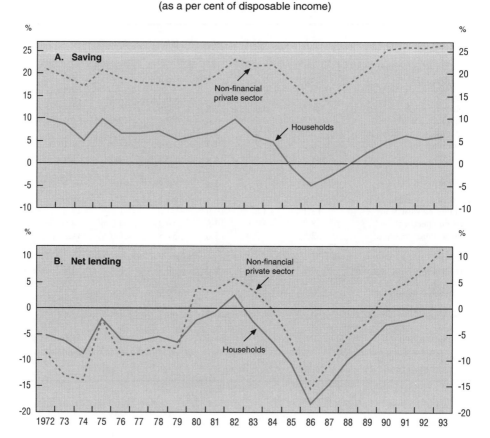

Source: Danmarks Statistik, *National Accounts;* Ministry of Economic Affairs.

The trend fall in residential construction came to a halt in early 1993: housing construction activity rose from the second quarter onwards, although it failed to regain its 1992 level for the year as a whole (Table 3). Housing starts were at an historical low in 1993, as high real interest rates and construction costs in excess of real-estate prices reduced the demand for new houses. The bulk of new construction was limited to publicly-supported housing, the rest of the new housing market remaining depressed, despite a pick-up in activity and prices in

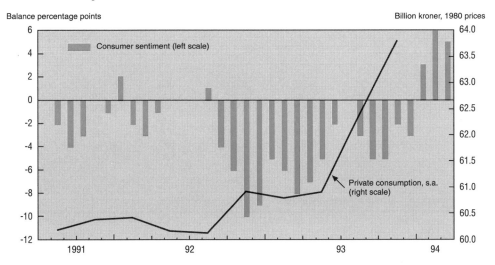

Diagram 4. **CONSUMER SENTIMENT AND PRIVATE CONSUMPTION**

Source: Danmarks Statistik, *Monthly review of statistics.*

the secondary market in the latter part of the year. This nascent recovery in the property market appears to have been driven by lower borrowing costs and government measures to encourage mortgage debt rescheduling (see below). As

Table 3. **The housing market and residential construction**

Year-on-year percentage changes

	1990	1991	1992	1993
New housing market				
Housing starts	−26.6	−22.3	−3.2	−27.8
Publicly supported	−22.7	−23.3	0.0	−16.7
Non-supported	−25.6	−20.3	−19.6	−46.3
Construction costs	5.3	3.3	2.4	2.4
Property market				
House prices	−7.5	1.3	−1.6	−0.9
Turnover	3.1	−7.7	−4.4	12.6
Forced sales	5.6	−14.7	−14.8	−14.8

Source: Økonoministeriet, *Økonomisk Oversigt.*

17

Table 4. **The commercial property market in Copenhagen: prices and rents**

DKr per square metre

	Offices		Shops		Industrial property	
	Price	Rent	Price	Rent	Price	Rent
1985	25 000	1 500	20 000	1 000	6 425	450
1986	25 000	1 500	21 500	1 075	6 786	475
1987	18 214	1 275	16 667	1 000	6 429	450
1988	16 857	1 180	15 833	950	5 313	425
1989	13 750	1 100	14 286	1 000	5 000	450
1990	12 500	1 000	12 143	850	4 722	425
1991	12 500	1 000	10 714	750	4 444	400
1992	10 286	900	6 875	550	3 590	350
1993	9 722	875	6 364	525	2 927	300

Source: International Commercial Property Associates, *International Property Bulletin* (various issues).

in the previous year, residential investment was also boosted by renovation and repair activity, such construction continuing to benefit from government subsidies.

Diagram 5. **CAPACITY UTILISATION AND INVESTMENT**

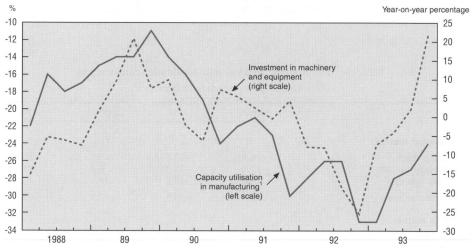

1. Difference between firms reporting excess capacity and firms reporting insufficient capacity.
Source: OECD.

18

The long-standing decline of fixed investment in commercial property gathered pace in 1993. In contrast to the residential sector, the commercial property market softened further (Table 4), although the fact that rents rose relative to prices increased the attractiveness of such property as an asset. Prices of shops and, in particular, industrial property in prime locations in the Copenhagen area have fallen below estimated construction costs, while the price of offices continues to exceed construction costs. A vacancy rate of 10 to 15 per cent is another sign of excess capacity in the office market.

Business equipment investment recovered in the course of 1993, despite spare capacity and high financing costs (Diagram 5). Such investment was boosted by strong capital spending by public utilities (in energy and communications) and purchases of transportation equipment. Despite the reduction in equipment investment prior to 1993, the stock of such capital goods has continued to expand relatively rapidly. For the most part, this reflects labour substitution rather than capacity-widening investment, deriving, at least in part, from a relatively low user cost of equipment.

Exports and imports

In spite of a strong rebound in the latter half of the year, export volumes fell in 1993 as a whole, as international demand weakened (Table 5). Moreover, in contrast to the significant market gains achieved in the 1990-1992 period, the export market share of Danish products stagnated (according to OECD estimates of market growth). Since, despite the appreciation of the krone, comparatively muted wage increases and strong gains in productivity allowed cost and price competitiveness to improve, the abrupt halt in market share gains cannot be ascribed to price/cost factors. It could, perhaps, have been related to the fact that the commodity composition of export demand was not as favourable as in earlier years, when international demand appears to have been directed at products in which Denmark specialises. Large volume reductions were recorded for exports of non-factor services, but this may be related to difficulties in dividing values into volume and prices.

Imports of goods and services fell by $4^1/_4$ per cent in volume in 1993 after stagnating in 1992 (Table 6). The year-on-year fall was much steeper than the decline in aggregate demand, the components registering the largest declines being particularly import-intensive so that import-weighted demand fell much

Table 5. Exports of goods and services

Percentage year-on-year change, 1980 prices

	1989	1990	1991	1992	1993
Total goods	5.3	4.7	5.9	5.0	0.3
of which:					
Manufactures [1]	9.2	5.9	6.3	6.0	n.a.
Oil and gas [1]	19.7	8.9	27.7	13.3	n.a.
Non-factor services	0.2	15.6	14.1	–0.6	–8.5
Total goods and services	4.2	6.9	7.7	3.7	–1.7
Memorandum items:					
Relative unit labour cost in manufacturing in common currency	–3.1	4.5	–3.4	1.0	0.5
Market growth, total goods	7.3	5.4	2.5	2.9	–0.7
of which:					
Germany	7.1	9.9	9.3	2.3	–9.6
Sweden	7.0	0.7	–6.0	–0.2	5.1
United Kingdom	7.9	1.3	–2.8	6.2	3.6
France	8.0	5.8	3.0	1.1	–3.5
Norway	–5.8	10.3	2.5	3.4	0.6
United States	4.4	2.4	0.5	10.4	11.6

1. Customs basis.
Source: Danmarks Statistik, *Statistisk månedsoversigt* (various issues); OECD.

Table 6. Imports of goods and services

Percentage year-on-year change, 1980 prices

	1989	1990	1991	1992	1993
Imports of goods	5.4	0.5	5.6	–0.4	–3.7
of which:					
Raw materials	2.8	2.8	1.8	5.3	n.a.
Energy	1.2	–4.7	6.2	1.2	n.a.
Capital equipment	1.0	6.9	0.9	–0.9	n.a.
Transportation	–1.6	8.3	7.7	4.3	n.a.
Consumer goods	6.3	5.9	10.4	4.4	n.a.
Imports of services	–0.1	5.1	0.8	–0.8	–7.0
Total goods and services	4.5	1.2	4.9	–0.5	–4.2
Memorandum items:					
Total domestic demand	0.5	–1.0	–0.5	–0.7	0.4
Import-weighted demand [1]	3.5	2.7	3.9	–0.1	–0.9
Goods consumption, excluding purchase of motor vehicles	–0.7	0.9	3.2	0.3	2.3

1. The import weights are from 1989.
Source: Danmarks Statistik, Input-output tabeller og analyser 1989, Copenhagen 1993; OECD.

20

more than total demand. Even allowing for this, however, import demand has been surprisingly weak, given the decline in import prices in both 1992 and 1993 and continued increases in prices on domestically-produced goods destined for the home market. As elsewhere in the EC, the figures for 1993 may be biased by under-recording.

Output, productivity and the labour market

Despite the recovery in aggregate output, total employment fell for the sixth consecutive year in 1993 (Table 7). Aggregate output and employment losses

Table 7. **Output, employment and productivity by sector**

Percentage changes from previous year

	1989	1990	1991	1992	1993
GDP at factor cost, total economy	**1.0**	**1.9**	**0.4**	**1.6**	**0.6**
Agriculture	8.1	0.8	−1.2	−6.7	28.5
Non-agricultural private sector	0.4	1.9	−1.2	1.5	−2.2
Mining and quarrying	21.6	2.4	19.7	6.6	2.5
Manufacturing	1.3	−1.1	−1.1	0.7	0.7
Electricity, gas and water	−1.5	7.8	−10.1	17.7	0.0
Construction	−6.9	−3.9	−14.5	−5.3	−5.0
Private services	1.2	3.6	0.7	2.0	−3.1
Public services	−2.9	−0.1	−0.1	0.6	2.9
Employment, total economy	**−0.6**	**−1.0**	**−1.8**	**−0.1**	**−0.5**
Agriculture	−4.6	−4.9	−5.0	−2.6	−1.8
Non-agricultural private sector	−1.3	−1.2	−2.1	−0.5	−2.1
Mining and quarrying	−4.0	−8.3	4.5	0.0	0.0
Manufacturing	−1.1	0.0	−1.5	−1.3	−4.0
Electricity, gas and water	4.2	−1.7	−0.6	1.2	−0.6
Construction	−6.0	−4.0	−5.3	−0.1	−2.2
Private services	−0.6	−1.3	−1.8	−0.1	−1.1
Public services	1.9	0.1	−0.6	1.0	2.7
Productivity, total economy	**1.6**	**2.9**	**2.2**	**1.7**	**1.1**
Agriculture	13.4	5.9	4.0	−4.2	30.9
Non-agricultural private sector	1.8	3.1	0.9	2.0	−0.1
Mining and quarrying	26.6	11.7	14.5	6.6	2.5
Manufacturing	2.4	−1.1	0.4	2.0	4.9
Electricity, gas and water	−5.5	9.7	−9.6	16.4	0.6
Construction	−0.9	0.1	−9.7	−5.2	−2.9
Private services	1.8	5.0	2.6	2.0	−2.1
Public services	−4.6	−0.2	0.5	−0.4	0.3

Source: Danmarks Statistik.

were moderated by expanding activity in the public sector, but the virtual stagnation of output in the private sector was associated with sizeable employment losses. The primary sector recorded unusually high output growth as crops returned to normal after the bad harvest of the previous year, but agricultural employment continued to drop. Output in the non-primary private sector declined and with it labour demand. Labour shedding in this sector was, however, comparatively light in relation to the output losses, and businesses appear to have reduced efforts to rationalise production processes in the downturn. The level of labour productivity consequently stagnated in the non-primary sector.

The evolution of output and employment differed across business sectors. The private service sector suffered output and employment losses in 1993, in contrast to earlier downturns when it had been largely insulated from the cycle. Output in this sector fell more than employment, suggesting an element of labour hoarding. Declining productivity levels were also recorded in construction, as employment reductions failed to keep pace with cuts in output. Productivity levels have been falling in the construction industry for several years, perhaps mirroring the shift away from ''high'' productivity new construction to ''low'' productivity renovation and repairs. Labour shedding was particularly steep in manufacturing, as a strong competitive environment and the appreciation of the krone forced firms to reduce costs. Labour productivity growth in manufacturing registered one of the highest rates for years.

Labour shedding has been reflected in a continued increase in unemployment (Table 8), one in eight workers being without a job in early 1994. Although the number of younger persons in the labour force remained on a downward trend, unemployment rates for the under 25 years old continued to rise. A contraction in the labour force of older persons was also accompanied by an increase in the rate of unemployment for workers above 60 years of age. Judging by the unemployment rates of members in occupational unemployment-insurance funds, skilled workers in many manufacturing industries and in construction appear to have been particularly hard hit by the recession (Table A1). The increase in joblessness has been more modest for clerical and office workers.

Table 8. **Labour force and unemployment by age**

	1989	1990	1991	1992	1993
A. Registered-based					
Labour force growth (per cent change)					
Total	–0.4	0.5	–0.3	0.0	0.7
Less than 25 years old	–5.8	0.2	–0.3	–3.9	–3.9
25 to 59 years old	2.0	–0.2	–0.2	0.9	1.3
More than 60 years old	–6.0	0.2	0.3	–1.6	–4.4
Unemployment rate[1]					
Total	9.5	9.7	10.6	11.4	12.4
Less than 25 years old	10.2	10.2	10.1	10.7	11.3
25 to 59 years old	9.3	9.6	10.8	11.7	12.9
More than 60 years old	8.7	9.2	9.0	8.8	9.3
B. Survey-based					
Labour-force growth, total	–1.4	1.0	0.2	n.a.	n.a.
Unemployment rate	8.8	8.8	9.8	n.a.	n.a.
Memorandum items:					
Population growth[2]					
17 to 24 years old	–1.2	–1.5	–2.1	–1.7	
25 to 59 years old	1.0	1.2	1.3	1.3	

1.   Registered unemployed persons as a percentage of the labour force.
2.   Growth in estimated mid-year population, the mid-year estimated as a simple average of populations at beginning and end of year.
Source: Danmarks Statistik, Statistisk månedsoversigt; Danmarks Statistik, Arbejdsmarked, Arbejdsstyrkeundersøgelsen; Danmarks Statistik, *Statistisk Årbog* (various issues).

Wages, prices and profit margins

The rise in unemployment has been accompanied by a further deceleration in wage increases, to the lowest rate for decades (Diagram 6). However, those in employment have continued to see gains in the purchasing power of their wages, amounting to 0.8 per cent in 1993 (Table 9). Measured against the evolution of product prices, the increase in wages has been even more pronounced, the willingness of businesses to raise real wages reflecting an increasingly favourable profit positions in recent years. The continued increase in real labour costs has done nothing to discourage the substitution of equipment for labour. Indeed, real wage increases in the face of high and rising unemployment rates suggest that the

Diagram 6. **WAGE INFLATION AND UNEMPLOYMENT**

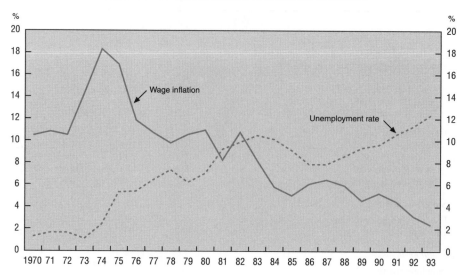

Source: OECD.

Table 9. **Wage developments**

Percentage change from previous year

	1989	1990	1991	1992	1993
Business sector					
Wage per person	4.5	5.2	4.4	3.1	2.3
Real consumption wage [1]	0.2	2.4	2.2	1.0	0.8
Real product wage [2]	−1.2	1.1	0.1	0.8	0.9
Labour productivity growth [3]	2.8	3.9	2.9	2.5	2.6
Manufacturing					
Hourly compensation	4.6	4.8	4.5	3.3	2.5
Real hourly product wage	−2.3	3.9	2.6	5.2	3.4
Hourly productivity	1.8	1.1	5.2	4.1	4.2
Construction					
Labour costs	0.9	2.7	3.4	2.5	3.3

1. Wages per person deflated by the implicit price deflator for consumption.
2. Compensation per person deflated by the implicit price deflator for business GDP.
3. Output per employed person.
Source: OECD; Danmarks Statistik, *Statistisk månedsoversigt.*

24

NAWRU, the unemployment rate needed to stabilise wage inflation, may have drifted up in the recent recession, and that it may currently exceed the officially-estimated 8 to 9 per cent level. This is further discussed in Part III.

The advance in the consumer price index remained subdued in 1993 (Diagram 7 and Table 10). Helped both by falling import prices in the wake of the effective appreciation of the krone and by reduced prices for farm products, the CPI net of taxes increased by only 1.4 per cent in 1993, decelerating throughout the year. Several products have fallen in price (Diagram 7). Indeed, more than a third of the product groups making up the consumer price index experienced stable or declining prices in the course of 1993, while a little less than a third registered increases in excess of 2 per cent. On the other hand, the decline in wholesale and producer prices showed a tendency to taper off in the course of 1993.

There is no evidence of profit margins being cut in the course of the recession, although the evolution of profit mark-ups has differed sharply across sectors (Table 11). Mark-ups in manufacturing have continued to increase, despite reportedly large spare capacity in that sector. Modest reductions in mar-

Table 10. **Consumer prices**

Percentage year-on-year change

	1989	1990	1991	1992	1993
Consumer price deflator	4.3	2.6	2.2	2.1	1.5
Consumer price index	4.8	2.6	2.4	2.1	1.2
of which:					
Goods	4.4	1.2	1.2	1.2	0.0
Services	4.4	4.2	3.5	3.4	2.4
Net price index [1]	5.2	3.1	2.6	2.1	1.4
Contribution in percentage points [2]					
Import prices, excluding energy	0.6	–0.4	0.2	0.0	–0.4
Energy	0.6	0.1	0.0	–0.3	–0.1
Agricultural products	0.2	–0.3	–0.1	0.0	–0.5
Rents	1.0	1.0	0.8	0.5	0.5
Public charges	0.5	0.3	0.4	0.3	0.2
Other domestic factors	2.4	2.4	1.3	1.6	1.7

1. Consumer prices excluding net indirect taxes.
2. The contributions are estimated by the Ministry of Economic Affairs.
Source: OECD; Økonomiministeriet, *Økonomisk Oversigt*, December 1993; Danmarks Statistik, *Prisstatistik* (various issues).

Diagram 7. **PRICE DEVELOPMENTS**

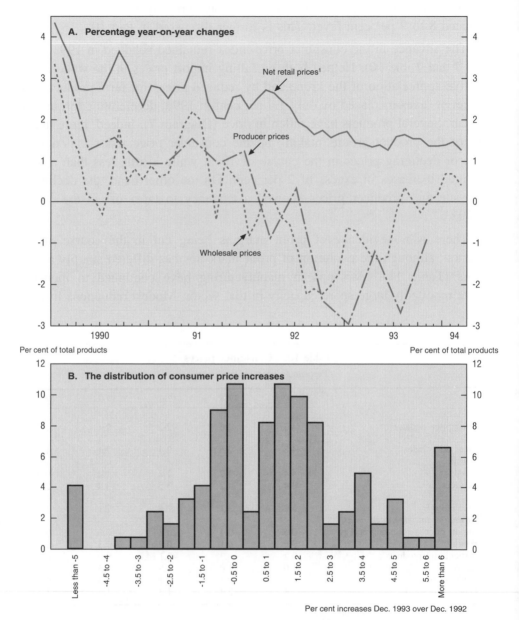

1. Net of indirect taxes and subsidies.
Source: Danmarks Statistik, OECD.

Table 11. **Profit mark-ups**[1]

	Manufacturing	Construction	Trade, etc.	Transportation	Business services	Private sector
1989	11.7	12.0	36.0	33.9	46.3	28.3
1990	11.9	12.0	36.4	38.0	47.9	29.4
1991	12.2	10.3	38.3	37.1	54.4	30.0
1992	13.6	11.0	41.8	37.3	56.5	31.1
1993	15.5	11.5	42.7	39.9	51.5	32.9

1. Operating profits as a percentage of labour and non-labour input costs.
Source: Danmarks Statistik, *Nationalregnskab*, various issues.

gins have, however, been recorded for business services, while margins in the recession-hit construction sector have risen modestly. Notwithstanding an apparent intensified competition from discount chains, profit mark-ups have increased in retail and wholesale trades.

The balance of payments

The current account registered a record surplus of 4 per cent of GDP in 1993 (Table 12). The improvement in the overall external balance was matched by larger surpluses on the trade account, which in turn reflected volume movements, the terms of trade for goods remaining unchanged. Significant terms-of-trade losses for non-factor services amplified the weakening of the real balance, but the deficit on the overall services balance remained broadly constant, thanks to lower debt-servicing charges. The strengthening of the investment-income balance reflected both lower international interest rates and declining foreign debt. Current account surpluses since 1990 have reduced the foreign debt as a percentage of GDP by some 9 percentage points, to around 31 per cent at the end of 1993.

Transactions on the capital account in 1993 were marked by the turbulence on currency markets. Huge capital exports by financial institutions reflected foreign borrowing in krone, in part to cover krone exposure on holdings of krone bonds, and the hedging by banks of forward contracts entered into with foreign investors. However, the non-bank private sector imported capital, notably through the sale of krone-denominated bonds, some of which was financed by

Table 12. **Balance of payments**

DKr billion

	1990	1991	1992	1993
Exports of goods, fob	222.4	234.9	245.1	241.9
Imports of goods, fob	192.3	204.6	201.8	191.0
Trade balance, fob	30.0	30.3	43.3	50.9
Exports of services	76.4	89.4	90.3	82.0
Imports of services	62.9	66.7	65.6	65.5
Services, net	13.5	22.7	24.7	16.5
Investment income	42.0	59.4	93.4	147.5
Investment expenditure	76.8	95.0	127.1	178.1
Investment income, net	−34.9	−35.6	−33.7	−30.6
Transfers, net	−0.4	−3.2	−5.5	−2.1
Current account	8.2	13.2	28.8	34.7
Public capital flows, net	8.4	−27.9	10.3	61.4
Private capital flows, net	23.0	2.6	−27.4	−73.0
Unrecorded capital movements, errors, etc.	−18.1	−8.7	−12.8	1.7
Total capital flows	13.3	−34.0	−29.9	−9.9
Change of exchange reserves	21.6	−20.8	−1.1	24.8
Memorandum items:				
Current account (per cent of GDP)	1.0	1.7	3.3	4.0
Foreign debt, net (per cent of GDP)		38.9	35.4	31.1
Terms of trade (per cent change)	0.3	−0.2	0.3	0.1
of which:				
Goods	1.0	−0.3	0.8	0.0
Services	−1.8	−1.3	−1.3	−3.3

Source: Danmarks Statistik; Danmarks Nationalbank.

krone-borrowing from banks. In addition to the surplus on the current account, net private capital exports were financed through official borrowing abroad. As such borrowing exceeded the required financing of net private capital exports, the authorities increased their foreign reserves accordingly.

II. Economic Policies

Since the autumn of 1992 the main focus of macroeconomic policy has been to bring down high unemployment. The monetary stance has, however, remained firm, as the commitment to a stable exchange rate came under pressure from repeated turbulence on foreign-exchange markets. Some easing in financial conditions has been possible since the widening of the ERM bands in August 1993, but the task of supporting demand has been assigned principally to fiscal policy. The easing of fiscal policy is to be temporary. As stated in the Danish convergence programme, the medium-term aim is to fulfil the Maastricht criteria of limiting public debt to 60 per cent of GDP and public deficits to 3 per cent of GDP. The authorities remain committed to this aim as an important element of policy in its own right, rather than as a preparation for stage III of the EMU, Denmark having given notification that it will not participate in this stage. Moreover, countercyclical action has been combined with important structural policy initiatives designed to enhance the growth potential of the economy.

Monetary policy and financial markets

Short-term interest rates and exchange rates

The year to August 1993 was marked by repeated disturbances on the foreign-exchange market, with temporary hikes in interest rates and large-scale intervention designed to keep the krone within the narrow band of the ERM (Diagrams 8 and 9). This turbulence was part of a general currency-market unrest, associated in Denmark's case with doubts about the ability of the authorities to maintain ERM parities at a time when there was pressure for interest rate cuts in order to support activity. To re-establish the credibility of the objective, following the floating of the Norwegian krone in December 1992, the authorities were forced to raise the short-term interest rates substantially, increasing the

Diagram 8. **INTEREST AND EXCHANGE RATE DEVELOPMENTS**

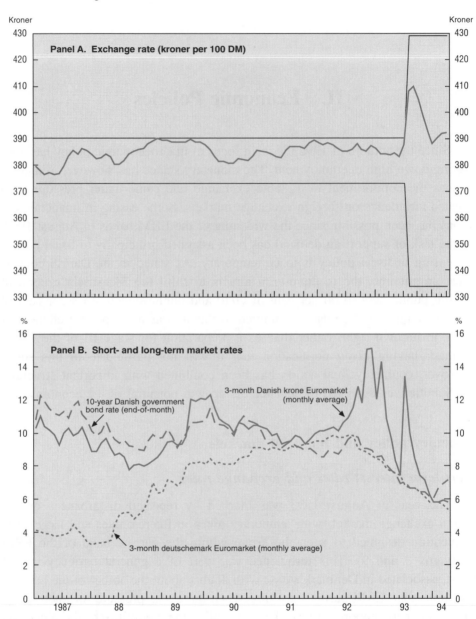

1. Rate of banks' borrowing at the Central Bank, end-of-month.
Source: Danmarks Nationalbank, OECD.

Diagram 9. **ADMINISTERED INTEREST RATES IN DENMARK AND GERMANY**

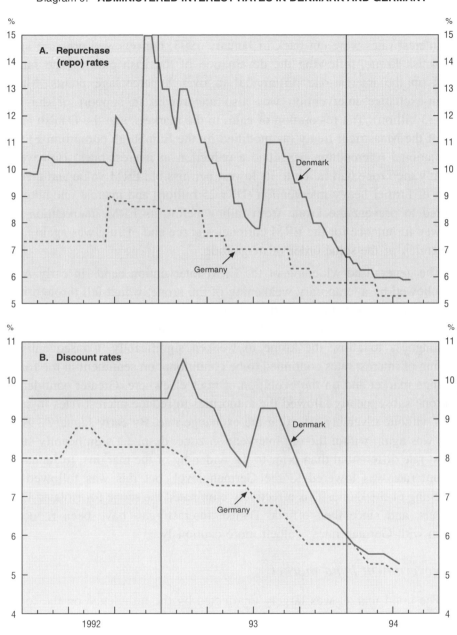

Source: OECD.

31

differential *vis-à-vis* Germany from less than 2 percentage points to around 7 percentage points.

Interest rates were cut back in January 1993, but renewed pressure against the Danish krone, following the devaluation of the Irish punt in late January, forced up the interest-rate differential to over 8 percentage points. Massive foreign-exchange intervention was also undertaken in support of the krone (DKr 33 billion). The restoration of calm in the markets, and the Danish acceptance of the Maastricht treaty (as modified by the Edinburgh compromise) in the June national referendum, permitted a reduction in interest rates. However, by mid-July the krone had fallen to its lowest permissible ERM value and a combination of further heavy intervention (DKr 25 billion) and interest rate hikes was required to prevent the krone from falling below its ERM intervention limit. Renewed turbulence for the ERM currencies at the end of July was again met by intervention of the same order of magnitude.

The generalised widening of the ERM intervention bands in early August was followed by a temporary weakening of the krone, which fell through its old ERM floor. However, the authorities restated their policy of not permitting any change in central rates *vis-à-vis* the core ERM currencies and signalled their unwillingness to allow the krone to weaken significantly. Consequently, the lowering of interest rates continued to be conditional on sentiment in the foreign-exchange market and on the evolution of rates elsewhere. Greater confidence in the krone subsequently allowed the authorities to reduce interest rates in several stages without adversely affecting the exchange rate. By early January 1994 the krone was again within the old intervention zone, despite a significantly smaller interest-rate differential than prior to the widening of the margins. In January the discount rate was lowered to the German level, but this was followed by a weakening of the krone. This effectively eliminated the scope for isolated Danish rate cuts, and since then official Danish interest rates have been reduced in tandem with German rates – albeit more cautiously.

The government bond market

The bond market was largely unaffected by the turbulence on the foreign-exchange market, yields on 10-year bonds falling by $2^{1}/_{2}$ per centage points in the year to January 1994. As in other OECD countries, yields have firmed more recently, reflecting an international trend rather than domestic considerations.

Overall, the net decline in yields has been larger at shorter maturities. As a consequence, the long-standing inverted yield curve for bonds with a life of two years or longer first flattened and then became positively sloped for the first time since 1989 (Diagram 10). For bonds and other financial instruments with a maturity of two years or less, the yield curve has remained inverted, though flattening. There was also a significant narrowing of the yield differential *vis-à-vis* Germany, with the widening of the gap in 1992 being reversed in the first half of 1993 (Diagram 11). From mid-1993 to early spring 1994 the yield differential fluctuated between 0.2 and 0.6 percentage points, but increased significantly in the second quarter.

Bank lending rates and monetary aggregates

Average lending rates for private borrowers peaked in the last quarter of 1992 at 12¼ per cent, and then declined by 1¾ percentage points over the first three quarters in 1993. At over 10 per cent, such rates imply very high real interest rates. At the same time, the spread between commercial bank lending and borrowing rates remained stable. The differential between lending rates and the discount rate at the Central Bank also remained stable at a high level despite some signs that increased competition among banks is putting pressure on margins. Improved operating costs have been required to counter continued high loan losses in the banking system (at 2½ per cent of the loan stock in 1993). Together with injection of new private capital this kept the risk-adjusted capital-adequacy ratio at 12.5 per cent, 3½ percentage points higher than the legal minimum. The capital position of the banking system thus remains fundamentally sound and in a much better state than in other Nordic countries, although the central bank was called upon to offer guarantees in connection with the closure of a few regional banks.

Growth in the money stock gathered momentum in the course of 1993 following a decline in the previous year (Table 13). However, bank loans fell for the third consecutive year, as high interest rates reduced loan demand and banks have also to some extent adjusted their lending policies to increased risks as reflected by high loan losses. The counterpart of the money growth was therefore external transactions, notably banks' acquisition of foreign currency in order to cover foreign-exchange exposure on customers' transactions in the forward exchange market and krone-denominated lending to finance purchases of krone-denomi-

Diagram 10. **TERM-STRUCTURE OF INTEREST RATES**

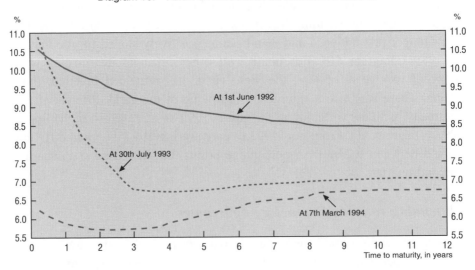

Source: Danmarks Nationalbank.

Diagram 11. **YIELD DIFFERENTIAL ON 10 YEARS BONDS**
Danish rate minus German rate

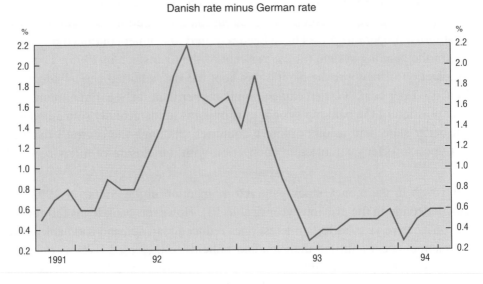

Source: Central Bank Quarterly Bulletin (various issues).

Table 13. **Money and credit**

Percentage year-on-year changes, end of period

	1990	1991	1992	1993	1993			
					Q1	Q2	Q3	Q4
Money stock	6.3	4.2	−1.2	11.4	0.2	2.8	6.3	11.4
Domestic credit creation	−2.5	0.8	−11.5	−12.3	−14.0	−14.2	−9.9	−12.3
Bank lending								
Total	8.0	−4.5	−0.8	−9.5	−5.6	−7.9	−6.9	−9.5
Businesses	9.3	−7.1	2.1	−7.9	1.1	−5.0	−3.5	−7.9
Non-businesses	6.0	−0.2	−5.3	−12.3	−17.9	−13.6	−13.2	−12.3
Mortgage bonds	3.2	3.6	0.6	17.8	0.5	1.7	4.6	17.8

Source: Central Bank.

nated bonds. As discussed above, these flows were related to the unrest on the foreign exchanges.

The mortgage bond market

A notable feature of financial-market developments in 1993 was increased lending by mortgage credit institutions, associated with enhanced opportunities to convert high-yielding bonds to lower-yielding bonds. The mortgage-bond market, which plays a dominant role in financing housing transactions, has been strongly influenced by government measures, aimed at stimulating the housing market. Conversion of existing high-yielding to new low-yielding bonds has been encouraged by modifications to tax rules, including the facility for borrowers to transfer the tax benefits associated with the higher yielding bond to new lower yielding ones. There has been great interest in converting such loans, as this reduces after-tax interest payments and permits a lengthening of repayment periods. All in all, mortgage bonds worth DKr 225 billion (equivalent to 25 per cent of GDP) were converted in the nine months to February 1994. In addition to the conversion itself, many households have used the opportunity to increase their mortgage debt and thus their liquidity. For the most part, however, conversion has transitory effects on the loan stock as new bonds are issued before the old bonds are retired. The very sharp increase of mortgage bonds in the last quarter of 1993 therefore significantly overstates the "underlying" lending expansion of the mortgage credit institutions, but it testifies to the popularity of converting mortgage loans.

Fiscal policy and tax reform

The fall in bond yields took place in the face of a significant easing of fiscal policy. Indeed, the announcement of reflationary measures in May 1993, following the referendum on the European Union, may even have helped strengthen the bond market, via market perceptions that, given a rather sound underlying fiscal stance and the temporary nature of the support measures, the credibility of foreign-exchange rate targets would be enhanced by supporting activity. Cyclically-induced increases in public deficits in the early 1990s had raised the general government deficit to 4 per cent of GDP in 1993 (Diagram 12) which was close to the average of OECD countries. But at only 1 per cent of GDP the estimated structural deficit was one of the lowest in the OECD area. With both the gross and net government debt position close to the average for the OECD (Diagram 13), a temporary fiscal expansion could thus be defended as consistent, over the medium-term, with the objective of meeting the fiscal criteria of the Maastricht Treaty.

Public finances in 1993 and 1994

The 1993 Budget was revised on several occasions in the course of the year. Measures taken in spring 1993 increased spending by DKr 0.3 billion, mainly on support to agriculture, fisheries, and housing. The subsequent reflationary programme was mainly directed at supporting activity in 1994 and beyond, but also contained measures which were to take effect in 1993. Initial plans were for a spending increase of DKr 1.6 billion: DKr 1.4 billion for public investment, housing and support to businesses; and DKr 0.2 billion for active labour-market policy (see below). In the event only DKr 650 million were appropriated during 1993: DKr 250 for renovation of state property and DKr 400 million for increased support to restoration and maintenance of private housing. Only minor measures were taken on the income side of the budget. The relaxation in 1993 is officially estimated to have contributed 0.6 percentage point to GDP growth in 1993.

Diagram 12. **GENERAL GOVERNMENT BUDGET BALANCES**

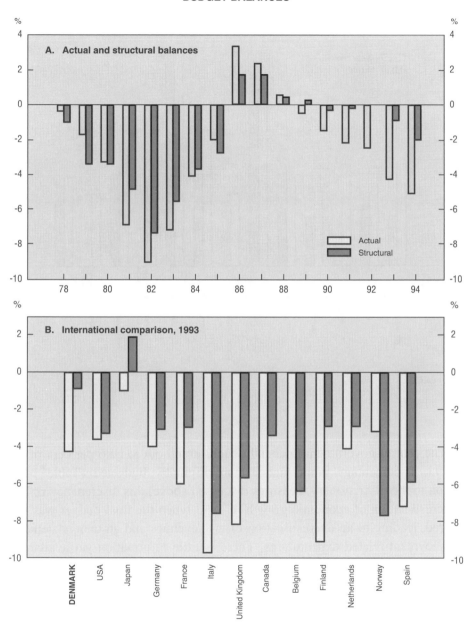

Source: OECD.

Diagram 13. **GENERAL GOVERNMENT DEBT, 1993**
Per cent of GDP

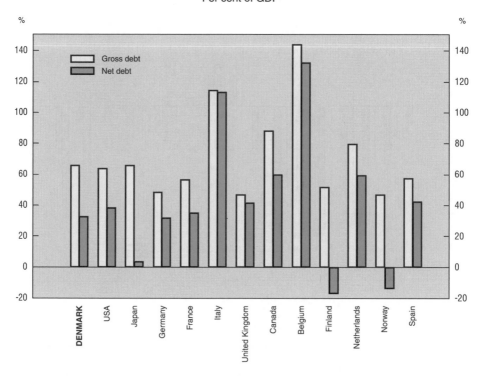

Source: OECD.

The central government financial deficit turned out to be 6 per cent of GDP in 1993, 1 percentage point higher than originally budgeted (Table 14). In addition to the discretionary measures discussed above, this discrepancy reflected an overestimation of economic growth in 1993 when the final budget was being prepared, leading to an overestimation of tax revenues and an understatement of unemployment-related expenditures. There is little information yet available on the outcome for local government finances in 1993. However, as a result of relaxation of borrowing constraints on local authorities to encourage infrastructure investment, their financial deficit is likely to be higher than budgeted. Early estimates suggest that local authorities may have increased such loan-financed spending by DKr 3½ billion. Public pension funds, which are classified as part of

Table 14. **Central government budget balances: expectations and outcomes**

Administrative basis, DKr billion

	1991		1992		1993		1994	
	Fiscal budget	Outcome	Fiscal budget	Outcome	Fiscal budget	Prelimi-nary out-come	Fiscal budget	Estimated outcome
Total income	282.6	279.8	297.8	295.1	307.4	310.9	334.5	338.9
of which:								
Direct taxes	128.8	124.8	125.0	123.1	131.8	137.3	140.2	142.9
Indirect taxes	145.1	141.9	157.2	155.0	161.4	154.8	176.6	177.0
Other	13.8	13.1	15.6	17.0	14.2	18.8	17.7	19.0
Total expenditure	312.1	318.2	326.3	333.0	351.3	359.3	388.9	389.9
of which:								
"Framework" spending	238.7	247.0	253.1	264.6	276.6	280.9	308.0	310.2
Interest payments	58.2	56.1	56.7	52.9	58.9	62.0	62.8	61.7
Other[1]	15.2	15.1	16.5	15.4	15.8	16.3	18.1	18.0
Financial balance	−29.5	−38.4	−28.5	−37.9	−43.9	−48.4	−54.4	−51.0
Financial balance, per cent of GDP	−3.5	−4.6	−3.3	−4.4	−4.9	−5.5	−5.9	−5.5

1. Child support and EC contributions.
Source: Finansministeriet, Budgetdepartementet, *Budgetoversigt* (various issues).

the general government according to national-accounts conventions, although in Denmark pension contributors have ownership rights to the accumulated assets, remained in a sizeable financial surplus.

The 1994 Fiscal Budget is marked by further stimulatory measures amounting to DKr 11 billion (1.2 per cent of GDP), which are officially estimated to boost GDP growth by 1¼ percentage points in 1994 when fully implemented. Spending increases (DKr 6¼ billion) are divided into four areas: labour-market initiatives and education (1.2 billion); growth-stimulatory measures (3.0 billion); special measures for children, health and culture (0.4); and other items (1.7 billion). Outlays could prove to be higher in the labour-market area, since the authorities' assumption that leave arrangements will be automatically financed through lower spending on passive support may not necessarily hold. On the income side the first stage of a five-year tax reform programme will involve a loss of revenue of some DKr 4.6 billion. The effect of these discretionary measures on actual budget balances will be masked by cyclical improvements, leaving the officially-estimated financial balance as a per cent of GDP unchanged from 1993. An agreement between central government and local authorities from June 1993 is for an unchanged tax rate in 1994. Their spending is budgeted to increase by 3 per cent from the 1993 Budget levels.

Counter-cyclical policy: effectiveness and efficiency

The effectiveness of stabilisation policy in a small open economy like Denmark is likely to be diluted by leakages into imports. The import/GDP ratio (0.33) is significantly higher than in the larger continental European countries (0.21 to 0.27), but somewhat lower than the average (0.36) of the smaller European countries. In contrast to most other countries the ratio has not increased over recent decades, suggesting a lower import elasticity of demand than elsewhere. But even so, a general fiscal expansion would not be likely to provide more than a partial stimulus to the economy. With this in mind the authorities have attempted to select the fiscal levers in order to achieve the maximum "first round" impact. Thus, certain of the stimulatory measures in the 1994 Budget are directed at sectors with heavy domestic content.

Even if fiscal policy has an appreciable impact on activity, however, the success of fiscal policy as a countercyclical device depends crucially on correct timing. The fiscal measures contained in the 1994 Budget had already been outlined in May 1993, and were included in the draft Fiscal Budget presented in August. Their implementation started only in January 1994. In the meantime, as noted in Part I, there are some indications that the economy has already entered a recovery phase. Because of lags in decision making, the budget measures will be to some extent pro-cyclical, although unemployment has nevertheless continued to increase through the first quarter of 1994. Moreover, by underpinning the rise in private sector confidence the early announcement of the 1994 fiscal measures may have contributed to the pick up in activity in 1993.

Fiscal consolidation

The eventual aim of fiscal policy is to eliminate net public debt, which currently stands at 35 to 40 per cent of GDP (see Annex I), and fulfilling the EMU convergence criteria is one step towards that end. Following the easing of fiscal policy in 1993 and 1994, the general government deficit is significantly higher than the EMU criterion but gross public debt is close to the target of 60 per cent of GDP. The temporary nature of many of the spending increases and the gradual phasing in of the tax reform should imply that the structural budget position will strengthen over the coming five years (Table 15). Moreover, if structural unemployment rates fall by 1½ percentage points in the second half of the decade, as is officially projected to result from the labour-market reform and increased emphasis on further education, the budget would move into a modest actual and structural surplus. In this case, the EMU budget criteria would be comfortably fulfilled, even on unchanged policy assumptions.

There is, however, considerable uncertainty about the future evolution of productive potential, and budget deficits could persist with unchanged policies. As discussed below, recent initiatives in the labour-market area have reduced labour supply, and their overall impact on the structural unemployment rate could be modest. Given the officially-estimated structural unemployment rate of 8 to 9 per cent, current plans for government spending and revenues would suffice to

Table 15. **Discretionary fiscal measures, 1994-1998**

DKr billion in constant 1993 prices

	1994	1995	1996	1997	1998
Cumulative expenditure increases	7.7	7.0	6.1	3.5	2.7
of which:					
Public investment, housing and business support	2.7	2.5	2.8	1.6	0.8
Active labour-market and education policy	1.0	1.6	1.7	1.6	1.5
Other initiatives	4.0	2.9	1.6	0.3	0.4
Cumulative revenue losses					
of which:					
Personal income tax	20.0	25.9	31.8	37.5	45.9
"Green" taxes	−2.6	−5.2	−7.7	−10.0	−12.2
Employees' social security contributions	−10.5	−13.4	−16.7	−20.5	−21.9
Other	−2.3	−3.1	−4.6	−6.6	−11.2
Total cumulative weakening of central government budget	12.3	11.2	8.9	3.9	3.3

Source: Ny kurs mod bedre tider, May 1993.

41

eliminate the structural deficit. However, the structural unemployment rate may currently be higher than assumed in the authorities' medium-term survey (see below), in which case a structural budget deficit would persist. Provided the structural deficit does not exceed 2 per cent the debt/GDP ratio would tend to fall, but progress would be slow. In this case, interest payments on public debt would continue to be an impediment to reducing Denmark's rather high tax burden.

Tax reform

The five-year tax reform which has just got underway is intended to reduce the distortions associated with a high average tax burden. The main features of the reforms, which are designed to be revenue-neutral in the long run, are:

- A gradual reduction in marginal tax rates on personal incomes for all income groups over the 1994-1998 period by 8 to 14 percentage points. The aim is to encourage work incentives and to reduce the implicit subsidy to credit-financed spending arising from interest deductibility;
- The introduction of payroll taxes to finance labour-market policy measures. The contribution rate for employees will increase from 5 per cent in 1994 to 8 per cent in 1997, while an employers' contribution will be introduced in 1997 at a rate of 0.3 per cent, increasing to 0.6 per cent in 1998. These taxes on gross income will finance in part the reduction in personal income taxes;
- A significant increase in "green" taxes. Excise duties on electricity use and fossil fuels will be increased sharply, and charges on water and waste water will be introduced;
- A broadening of the tax base, by eliminating special privileged tax arrangements for some types of income;
- Introduction of progressive taxes on investment income and capital gains after a certain level has been reached.

The tax reform programme marks a significant overhaul of the structure of the tax system. The combined marginal rate of personal income tax and social security contributions will be lowered by 6 to 9 percentage points for most employees (Diagram 14).[2] By 1998 the combined marginal tax and contribution rate for the average production worker will have fallen to about the 1992 OECD average. However, the comparatively low employers' social security contribu-

Diagram 14. **MARGINAL TAX RATE SCHEDULES**

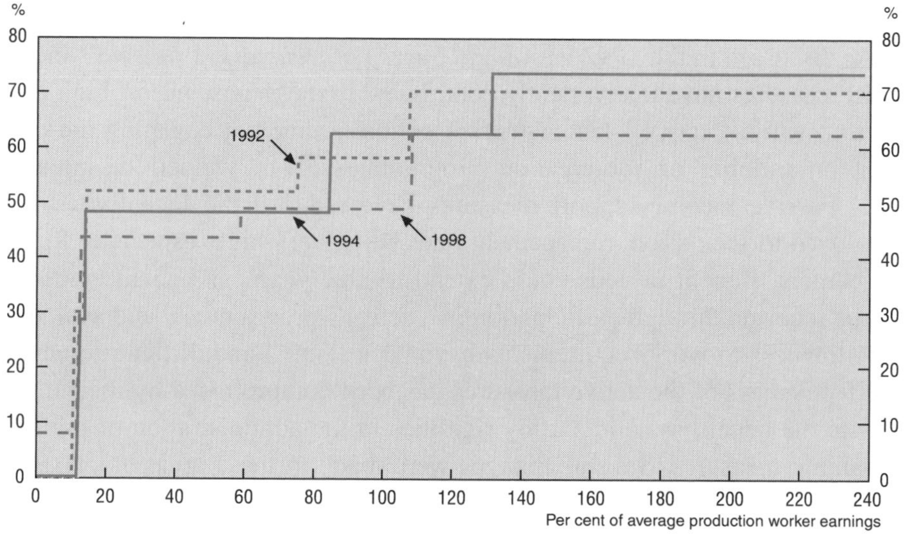

Per cent of average production worker earnings

Source: OECD.

tions in Denmark imply that the marginal tax imposed directly on the employee is still relatively high. This would seem to be especially significant for low-income earners, such as part-time workers, since the supply of such workers seems to be particularly sensitive to changes in tax rates.

Taxation of investment income and outlays will be subject to special rules under the new system. Interest income will be taxed like earned income with the exception of the top tax rate, which is to be subject to an additional capital-income allowance of DKr 20 000. Although the top marginal rate on investment income will still be 58.5 per cent, this applies only to a limited group of taxpayers. But to mitigate the impact of lower tax-deductibility of interest on the cost of housing finance, the imputed income from owner occupation is to be lowered from 2.5 to 2 per cent of the housing value, up to a certain limit. Official estimates suggest that the long-run impact of these last two measures on housing demand will offset each other.

Labour-market policies

As discussed in the *1992/93 Annual Survey of Denmark*, "passive" income-support measures have inadvertently contributed to the persistence of high unemployment, while "active" labour-market policies, aimed at engaging the unemployed on training or job-creation programmes, have yielded disappointing results. Passive income-support measures have reduced the incentives for the unemployed to seek a job, replacement rates being very high, especially for low-wage earners. Benefit periods could extend to nine years, as benefit entitlement could be renewed through participation in "active" programmes[3] and availability and willingness-to-work requirements have been "soft" and difficult to enforce. The effectiveness of the active measures has been compromised by their interaction with the benefit system, and by rigidities in the administration of job offers and training measures. Several changes were made in these areas as of 1994.

"Active" and "passive" policies

Government initiatives have been aimed at offering more timely help to vulnerable groups, concentrating active measures on the very long-term unemployed, and making their administration more flexible. The possibility of renewing entitlements by participation in active programmes has been abolished.[4] The increased emphasis on "active" programmes has been accompanied by a decentralisation of policy implementation to regional labour-market authorities, which have a large degree of freedom to adjust programme design to fit local needs.

It remains to be seen to what extent this package will have positive effects on employment prospects for the unemployed. The maximum benefit period is still very long by international standards. Moreover, as workers may earn the right to continued support through working for only six months, the possibility of cycles of long unemployment spells and short spells in employment remains, although participation in active measures no longer renews benefit rights. The preparation of individual action plans is likely to identify individuals at risk of very long spells at an early stage, but administrative difficulties may arise in the short run as plans have to be made for a very large number of people. Reduced sanctions for rejecting job offers may also make enforcement of availability and willingness-to-work requirements more difficult. The increased emphasis on

44

active measures should help to reduce unemployment in the long run, provided regional labour councils succeed in delivering relevant training courses.

Paid-leave arrangements

Paid leave arrangements have been changed to encourage people to take sabbatical leaves or leaves for education and child rearing (Table 16). The purpose of the schemes is to increase rotation in the labour market in order to reduce structural unemployment in the long run, and to enhance the skills of the work force. Leave for child rearing also aims at improving the situation of families with young children. The temporary arrangements for education and child-rearing leaves, introduced in 1992, pursued the objective of job rotation by making public support conditional on the regular worker being replaced by an unemployed person. This obligation is judged to have been unduly bureaucratic, reducing employers' interest in the schemes, with little impact on total replacement. It has therefore been abolished in the new education and child-minding schemes effective for three years from January 1994. Moreover, the unemployed themselves can now take advantage of paid-leave arrangements, and such leaves are not counted in maximum support periods for the unemployed. Compensation levels in these schemes are 80 per cent of maximum unemployment-insurance benefits,[5] which makes them particularly attractive for lower-paid workers. Indeed, the compensation rate can be even higher in child-minding leaves, as local authorities can supplement the compensation paid by the state.[6] There has been strong interest in the new schemes, and the authorities' original projections

Table 16. **Paid leave arrangements for employed and unemployed**

	Maximum length	Percentage of maximum unemployment insurance benefits	Eligibility criteria		
			Insured	Employment length	Age
Education leave	1 year	80[1]	Yes	3 years	> 25
Child-minding leave	1 year per child	80[2]	No	n.a.	n.a.
Sabbatical leave	1 year	80	Yes	3 years	> 25

1.   100 per cent until April 1995.
2.   Local authorities can provide supplements of up to DKr 35 thousand.
Source: Finansministeriet, Budgetdepartementet, Forslag til Finanslov for finansåret 1994.

of 20 thousand full-time participants is likely to be exceeded by a considerable margin.

While potentially encouraging skill acquisition, the schemes may have unwanted side-effects. Firstly, the unemployed have shown a great interest in such schemes, suggesting that they may be using them to lengthen maximum support periods. Second, the people taking leave may be in short supply, and therefore difficult to replace. Anecdotal evidence suggests that the leave schemes have been particularly popular among health-care workers in the public sector, threatening to close some wards. As discussed in Part III, the assumed participation in these schemes has important implications for the short-run projections.

Other measures

Other recent or prospective measures directly affecting the labour market include:

- *The temporary subsidisation* of home services, such as cleaning and gardening, as from January 1994, aimed at creating jobs for low-skilled workers and reducing the extent of "black" work in these areas. The subsidy involves a fixed amount (DKr 65 later increased to DKr 85) per hour, and DKr 1 billion has been allocated to this programme in the Budget.
- *Education initiatives*, including the creation of 20 thousand new places in education institutions in 1994. Half of the increase will be in ordinary establishments, and half in adult education programmes.
- *New regulations on shop opening hours*, as of March 1994, aiming at clarifying existing rules and extending standard opening hours to 8 p.m. Some restrictions were established on the sale of goods in convenience stores outside normal shopping hours.
- A planned tightening of *collective dismissal legislation*, lengthening notice periods for blue-collar workers to eleven weeks from 30 days currently stipulated. This change, which builds on an EC directive from 1992, will only apply to establishments with more than 100 employees laying off more than 50 per cent of the workforce.

The education initiatives should help to upgrade the skills of the workforce and improve employment prospects as long as the expansion is directed at skills in short supply. However, as discussed in Part IV, subsidies to home services are unlikely to reduce labour costs sufficiently to create many additional jobs, given the high wages of low skilled workers. Moreover, there would seem to be some scope for the misuse of this system. As the tightening of employment protection legislation will be applied to only few workplaces, it is unlikely to have much adverse effect on hirings.

III. The Short-term Outlook: Challenges and Risks

Most recent conjunctural indicators suggest that a vigorous upturn is already underway. Private consumption appears to have picked up markedly, as an unusually rapid and steep improvement in consumer confidence has accompanied the upturn. And the firming of the housing market in the course of 1993 has recently shown up in stronger residential construction. Surveys register a marked increase in optimism in the business sector as a whole. A robust output expansion is expected to continue over the coming two years. The challenge will be to translate the current growth momentum into a sustained medium-term expansion, given the risks that consumption could respond more strongly than expected, or that the supply response may be inadequate.

The short-term outlook

Economic policy assumptions and the external environment

The overall stance of macroeconomic policy is set to be expansionary in the short term (Table 17). Basing fiscal policy assumptions for 1994 on the Budget and those for 1995 on stated policy intentions, the fiscal stance will be expansionary in 1994, moving towards restraint in 1995. With short rates following the projected decline in German rates, the fiscal stimulus is likely to be amplified by accommodating monetary policy. The average real short-run interest rate in 1994 could drop by as much as 5 percentage points compared with 1993, and a further decline of 1½ percentage points is projected for 1995. However, long-term interest rates, which have far greater impact on economic activity, may only fall marginally, given the projected evolution of German bond yields.

48

Table 17. **Economic policy assumptions and the external environment**

	1993	1994	1995
Fiscal policy			
General government financial balance (per cent of GDP)	–4.5	–4.3	–3.2
Change in general government financial balance (per cent of GDP)	–2.1	0.2	1.1
of which:			
Cyclically-adjusted	–1.5	–1.1	0.1
Interest and exchange rates			
Effective exchange rate (1991 = 100)	105.1	104.4	104.6
Three-month German rates	7.3	5.1	4.3
Three-month domestic rates	10.3	5.8	4.8
Ten-year domestic bond yield	7.2	7.0	6.6
Export-market growth for manufactures			
Total	–0.7	4.7	6.7
Germany	–11.7	0.6	6.0
United Kingdom	3.0	5.9	7.7
Sweden	5.3	4.9	6.2
Norway	–1.0	4.2	5.9
Unit-labour cost growth in competitor countries			
Germany	3.6	–1.3	0.2
United Kingdom	0.2	1.5	1.6
Sweden	–1.5	0.0	0.9
Norway	–1.0	1.0	1.8

Source: OECD.

Aggregate demand should be further supported by a gradual recovery in the world economy. OECD projections from May show the area-wide GDP growth increasing from 1¼ per cent in 1993 to 2½ per cent in 1994 and 3 per cent in 1995. While import demand is likely to be sluggish in the important German market in 1994, renewed growth in European Member countries in general, and buoyant import growth in neighbouring Scandinavian countries in particular, should permit a sizeable expansion of export markets for Danish products, perhaps reaching an annual rate of 6¾ per cent. Moreover, on the technical assumption of unchanged exchange rates, projected unit labour cost trends will imply that Denmark's relative cost competitiveness could improve somewhat over the projection period.

The outlook for 1994 and 1995

Rapid real income growth should drive aggregate demand and output growth to well above potential rates in both 1994 and 1995 (Table 18). The fiscal measures outlined above will add around $2^{1}/_{2}$ to 3 per cent to household real disposable income, while private consumption could also be boosted by a declining household saving ratio, as improved net wealth reduces the need for saving out of current income. The recovery in both private consumption and foreign demand should, in turn, prompt an increase in business fixed investment, which would be reinforced by some further reduction in real interest rates. Capital

Table 18. **Short-term outlook**

Percentage changes from previous year

	1992	1993	1994[1]	1995[1]
Private consumption	0.7	2.6	5.3	3.8
Public consumption	0.7	3.2	1.3	0.4
Gross fixed investment	−8.2	−1.8	6.6	6.7
Business	−12.1	−3.6	7.5	8.3
Residential	−4.1	−3.1	3.8	6.2
Public	10.7	9.0	6.0	0.0
Final domestic demand	−0.9	2.0	4.4	3.4
Changes in stockbuilding[2]	0.2	−1.5	1.0	0.5
Total domestic demand	−0.7	0.4	5.5	4.0
Foreign balance	1.9	0.8	−1.0	−0.2
Exports	3.7	−1.7	4.0	5.5
Imports	−0.5	−4.2	8.0	7.2
Gross domestic product	1.2	1.2	4.0	3.5
Household saving ratio[3]	5.4	6.0	5.1	3.1
Private consumption deflator	2.1	1.5	2.0	2.6
GDP deflator	2.0	1.7	2.3	2.5
Current account balance, per cent of GDP	3.3	4.0	2.9	2.9
Total employment	−0.1	−0.6	1.2	0.9
Labour force	0.7	0.6	0.1	0.4
Unemployment rate[4]	11.2	12.2	11.0	10.5

1. OECD projection.
2. As a per cent of GDP in the previous year.
3. Level, per cent of household disposable income.
4. Level, per cent of labour force.
Source: OECD.

spending is, however, likely to be concentrated on equipment; the current excess supply of commercial property will damp expansion of business structures for years to come. Moreover, notwithstanding increased exports in the wake of the recovery in the world economy, the growth contribution from the real foreign balance is likely to be negative, because of the demand-driven increase in imports.

GDP is expected to grow at an annual rate of 4 and 3½ per cent in volume in 1994 and 1995 respectively. The pick-up in economic activity over the projection period is likely to increase total employment for the first time since 1987. The projections for the labour market are based on the assumption of 40 thousand people (1½ per cent of the labour force) participating in paid-leave schemes on average in 1994 and 1995: half entering these programmes from employment and half from unemployment. Participation in leave schemes will reduce the number of persons seeking work and hence the labour force. Of the employed persons going on leave three quarters are assumed to work in the public sector, of which a half are expected to be replaced. Only minor replacement is assumed for workers in the private sector going on leave. The combination of reduced labour supply and growing labour demand will reduce the unemployment rate significantly in 1994, with a further, more modest, reduction in 1995 arising from expanding employment.

Price increases are likely to remain moderate, although the inflation rate will exceed the 1993 level, which was influenced by the appreciation of the krone. The slack in the labour market, albeit diminishing, should ensure that the 1995 wage bargaining round results in moderate settlements. However, with the unemployment rate falling below 10½ per cent in 1995, some pressures in the labour market could emerge towards the end of the projection period.

Possible pressure points: household spending and supply constraints

The central projections are based on the assessment that the output gap – the gap between actual and potential output – is sufficiently wide that the projected increases in spending can be met without significant inflationary pressures emerging. There are, however, two major uncertainties: *i)* the evolution of household saving ratios and *ii)* the degree of labour-market slack available over the projection period. The experience from the 1980s showed that the saving ratio can drop sharply in a short time period, thus boosting demand growth significantly, while inflationary pressures may emerge at much higher level of unemployment than expected. A particular concern is that the leave schemes may lead to a policy-induced reduction in the growth of productive potential at a time when demand growth is being boosted.

Household finances and consumer spending

The reduction in the household saving ratio in the OECD projections is driven by the current and prospective improvement in the liquidity and financial asset position of households. Liquidity in the private sector has increased as a result of the opportunity to lengthen repayment periods – and increase the amount – of outstanding mortgage loans, weakening the incentives to save out of current income. Moreover, in the current environment of low inflation there is less need to save to make up for the inflation-induced loss of value of financial assets fixed in nominal terms, so that a decline in the saving ratio may be expected despite the fact that the current household saving ratios are low compared with the pre-1980s standard of 5 to 10 per cent. In any case, the saving ratio of the private sector as a whole is at a historically high levels. Since the ultimate owners of businesses are households, the high saving ratio in the corporate sector could and should influence spending by households.

Data on households' net wealth illustrate that the ratio of total wealth of households (excluding pension wealth) to disposable income in the course of the 1980s has fluctuated around a stable mean (Diagram 15), suggesting that saving falls if asset values increase relative to income (and *vice versa*). At the end of 1992 the ratio was close to its average level, and changes in asset prices and saving in the course of 1993 are likely to have increased the ratio well above the normal level. Prospects of higher property prices in the wake of lower interest rates will further boost wealth. Taking pension wealth into account, the wealth to income ratio is probably at a historically high level, and very much higher than prior to the 1980s upswing.

The need to renew ageing durable household equipment could also prompt a reduction in the measured household saving ratio. As in many other OECD countries, there is evidence of cycles of consumer durables purchases in Denmark (Diagram 16). A cyclical peak was reached in 1975/76 and again in 1983/84 , with corresponding troughs in 1980 and in 1987/88 . In the early 1990s

Diagram 15. **HOUSEHOLD FINANCES**
As a per cent of disposable income

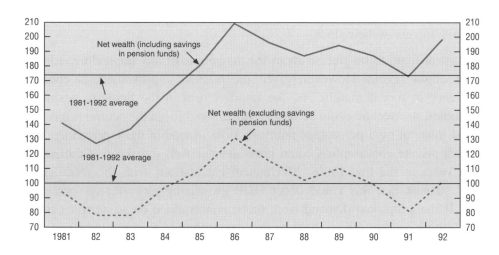

Source: Ministry of Economic Affairs.

Diagram 16. **PRIVATE CONSUMPTION**
Percentage change, 1980 prices

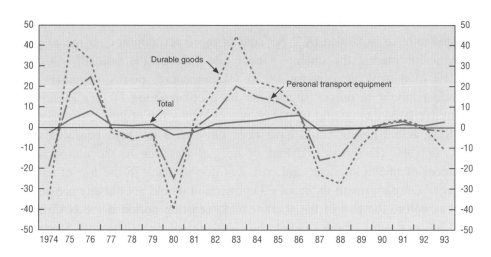

Source: Danmarks Statistik.

there was some pick-up in the purchases of consumer durables but the subsequent slump appears to have delayed further renewal of equipment. Consequently, the average age of durables has increased markedly, providing consumers with an incentive to renew their stock.

It is difficult to be precise about the magnitude of any impending reduction in household saving. However, given the marked improvement in consumer confidence in recent months and the improvement in the liquidity position of households, the decline could be faster than allowed for in the central projections. Should it be cut by 3 percentage points in 1994 instead of the 1 percentage point adopted, private consumption could grow at rates well in excess of those in the boom years in the mid-1980s. Mechanical calculations with the INTERLINK model suggest that this could boost GDP growth by more than 1 percentage point. If the additional demand were to be concentrated on passenger cars and other foreign-produced household equipment, activity effects could be somewhat smaller than this calculation suggests. Nonetheless, a very rapid increase in consumer spending could put labour and product markets under excessive strain.

Productive potential: emerging constraints

The OECD projections are based on the assessment of a substantial output gap in 1993. Notwithstanding falling gross investment levels, the capital stock is estimated to have expanded by 2 per cent or more per annum over recent years. In the labour market the unemployment rate exceeds the officially-estimated NAWRU of 8 to 9 per cent by $3\frac{1}{2}$ to $4\frac{1}{2}$ percentage points, suggesting that insufficient labour resources should not be a constraining factor. Taking into account available capital and labour resources (using the official estimate of the NAWRU), actual output could have been close to 5 per cent below potential output[7] in 1993 (Diagram 17). Part of he gap was due to the non-structural component of unemployment, and part was due to slack in the use of existing resources.[8] Output growth in the OECD projection would not put any pressure on resources before the end of the short-term forecasting period if the NAWRU is indeed $8\frac{1}{2}$ per cent: labour-market slack offsetting any inflationary tendencies emanating from capacity constraints. However, even in this case, the speed at which joblessness is falling, and pressures on capacity growing, could threaten to increase inflation.

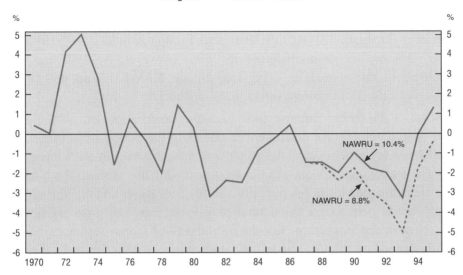

Diagram 17. **OUTPUT GAPS**

Source: OECD.

The availability of capital may also be less than recorded, as capital may have been prematurely scrapped in the course of the prolonged downturn. This would not be detected in capital-stock data compiled by using the perpetual inventory method with constant scrapping rates. The fact that manufacturing firms reported capacity utilisation rates in the latter part of 1993 having returned to levels prior to the recession could be taken as evidence of accelerated scrapping, given the gross investment which has taken place. Also, the hesitancy of profit mark-ups to decline in the downturn could signal that productive capacity may have weakened. True, even if physical capital has been prematurely scrapped in the downturn, the remaining capital may be used more efficiently, for example by greater use of shift work, but rigidities in work organisation could make the availability of capital a constraint on output expansion in the short run.

There are also considerable uncertainties about the current structural unemployment rate, and the 8½ per cent level mentioned above may have been overtaken by events. Experience from several OECD countries would seem to suggest that increases in unemployment rates can turn into structural increases.

55

Indeed, the structural unemployment rate, as recently measured by the OECD, rose during the late 1980s, so that by 1992 it was close to or even exceeded 10 per cent (Diagram 18). At this level actual output would have been around 3½ per cent below potential output in 1993. However, by 1995 the actual unemployment rate would be very close to the NAWRU, and pressures on existing capacity could prompt inflationary tendencies.

Some of the recent labour-market measures could also increase the natural rate of unemployment. As noted above, extending the period of advance notice for collective lay-offs could make employers more hesitant in their hiring decisions. The weakening of work-availability tests could also push up the NAWRU. While the increased emphasis on timely "active" measures and on education and training should help to get the natural rate down, this will probably not have much effect in the short term. But the availability of labour resources will also critically depend on the increase in the "underlying" labour force. To the extent that it responds more elastically to the improvement in the labour market than projected, the danger of inflationary pressures will be lessened.

Diagram 18. **ACTUAL AND STRUCTURAL UNEMPLOYMENT**

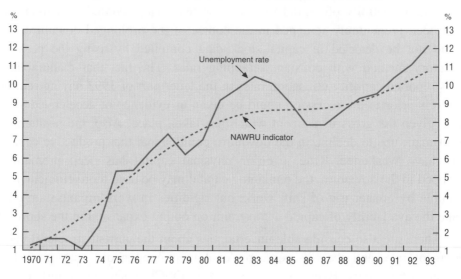

Source: OECD.

The availability of labour resources will particularly depend on how extensively the paid-leave arrangements will be used, and the extent to which those on leave are replaced. The assumption used in the OECD projections, that 40 thousand people will be on such schemes on average in both 1994 and 1995, is realistic given the contracts already signed in 1994. A similar participation rate is assumed in the latest official projections. Should there be no reduction in the number of new contracts signed per week in the course of the year, up to 60 thousand people could be on leave schemes on average in 1994. A further assumption underlying the projections is that employed workers going on leave are mainly in the public sector, and that only half of these workers are replaced. This implies that potential labour resources available to businesses are less affected than if all public workers on leave were to be replaced.

Different assumptions concerning the popularity of the leave schemes and the extent of replacement would have a significant impact on the output gap and thereby on inflationary pressures. Mechanical calculations of output gaps with different assumptions are presented in Table 19. As can be seen from the table, should the public sector keep "effective" employment levels constant, the resulting decline in potential labour resources available to the private sector would imply a significant rise in the ratio of actual to potential output. Significant

Table 19. **Output gaps[1] and leave arrangements: different assumptions**

	NAWRU = 10.4%		NAWRU = 8.8%	
	1994	1995	1994	1995
Assumptions				
Reference scenario:				
40 thousand participants, 50 per cent replacement in public sector	–0.1	1.3	–1.8	–0.4
Alternative scenarios:				
40 thousand participants, 100 per cent replacement in public sector	0.2	1.6	–1.6	–0.2
60 thousand participants, 100 per cent replacement in all sectors	0.9	2.3	–0.9	0.5

1. The output gap is defined as $q - q^*$, where q is business sector GDP and * denotes potential output. As mentioned in footnote 8 the output gap is equal to the sum of the gap between actual and normal output ($q - q^n$), and the gap between normal and potential output ($q^n - q^*$). The latter component depends on the difference between the actual unemployment rate and the NAWRU.
Source: OECD.

inflationary pressures could start emerging in 1994 if the NAWRU is 10.4 per cent. Even taking the official estimate of the NAWRU, the output gap could be virtually closed if it is assumed that all those going on leave from the public sector were replaced. In this case, should the uptake of the leave schemes be 60 thousand or more rather than the assumed 40 thousand, pressures on resources could become serious in 1995.

IV. The Business Sector: Performance and Policies

The economic conditions facing the Danish business sector are in many respects rather favourable, given low inflation, a stable exchange rate and low interest rates, and the turnaround in the external account which has accompanied fiscal consolidation and higher private-sector saving since 1986. While competitiveness problems were severe in the early 1980s, Denmark has gained export market shares since 1987. Structural reforms, particularly competition law reform and deregulation of the financial service industry, postal services, telecommunications and transport, have enhanced competition in the domestic market and tax reform has gone some way towards reducing work disincentives of high marginal tax rates. The participation rate is high and the ''non-employment'' rate low compared with other OECD economies. The weakest aspect of Danish economic performance is that, since 1986, employment growth has taken place only in the public sector, and persistently high structural unemployment has caused concern for the growth potential of the Danish economy.

The aim of this chapter is to identify the structural and institutional factors behind this apparent deficiency of private sector dynamism, as they relate to business-sector organisation and behaviour and the related industrial policy environment. The first part looks at business-sector structure and performance, the coverage being broadly defined to include manufacturing, construction and private traded services: Denmark shares with other OECD economies the characteristic that growth in manufacturing tends to derive from productivity gains rather than employment, so that the challenge is to create a wide range of jobs in non-manufacturing industries. The second part discusses the industrial and trade policy background, which has, on the whole, been liberal and non-interventionist; the third discusses recent policy developments, in the light of the current agenda for increasing the role of the state in promoting business-sector development, while the final section presents an assessment of policy needs.

Structure and performance of the Danish business sector

Structural characteristics

The Danish business sector[9] is smaller as a proportion of total value added and employment than in most other OECD countries (Table 20). Moreover, the share of industrial production in overall business sector output is comparatively limited, with manufacturing production based on an unusually large share of food and beverages – the offshoot of a traditionally strong agricultural sector. A corollary is that the Danish business sector contains a larger service element than the average. Moreover, by European standards, its share of services in total exports is relatively high. The Commission of the European Community (1993) reports that Denmark accounts for 5 per cent of intra-EC export of services – well above its share of merchandise exports – partly associated with the traditional strength of the sea transport sector.

Size distribution of enterprises

Partly due to the high share of service companies, the business sector is characterised by a high proportion of small and medium-sized enterprises compared with many other European countries (Table 21). Moreover, studies of consolidated company data for the Nordic countries show that in 1992, in terms of both sales and employment, no Danish corporation was among the top 15.[10] The comparative lack of larger companies can, however, be attributed to the size disadvantage of the country which is only partially offset by recourse to the export market (Diagram 19). Exports of goods and services correspond to around 27 per cent of GDP which is not high for a small OECD country.

The rate of new business formation in Denmark has been of some concern in recent years, corresponding to 5 per cent of the total of companies compared with around 10 per cent in most other northern European countries in 1990.[11] This might suggest a business sector with a relatively weak entrepreneurial culture. The picture is, however, far from clear in this regard: prior to the recession, the number of start-up companies was similar, as a per cent of total enterprises, to

Table 20.　**The structure of the Danish business sector**

Share of total business sector, 1992

	Employment	GDP[1]	Exports[2]
Manufacturing	31.2	25.6	77.2
of which:			
Food and beverages	5.4	5.2	7.6
Wood and paper	5.4	4.3	2.7
Chemicals	3.1	3.8	11.1
Machines and equipment	12.9	8.9	32.2
Construction	9.9	7.6	..
Tradeable services	57.1	65.8	22.8
of which:			
Retail and wholesale	17.4	17.6	..
Transport	8.7	9.6	..
Financial services	6.4	3.9	..
Business services	8.8	9.5	..
Household services[3]	5.5	4.2	..
Home services[4]	1.8	1.0	..
Memorandum items:			
Business sector share of total economy[5]			
Denmark	**64.2**	**73.0**	**..**
OECD[6]	73.5	81.2	..
Public sector as a share of total economy[5]			
Denmark	**30.4**	**21.5**	**..**
OECD[6]	18.7	13.4	..
Agriculture and fishing as a share of total economy[5]			
Denmark	**5.6**	**3.9**	**..**
OECD[6]	5.4	2.7	..

1.　At factor cost.
2.　Not including service exports from the construction sector.
3.　Including auto repairs.
4.　Including charitable institutions.
5.　1990.
6.　Largest eleven OECD economies.
Source: OECD, *National Accounts.*

other OECD economies, and it was high in relation to the population.[12] On the other hand, the Danish start-up figure is probably artificially raised by government subsidies to unemployed persons establishing new companies: a labour market-related scheme which has been in place for some years offers a monthly subsidy of 50 per cent of the maximum benefit level to unemployed persons

Table 21. **Distribution of business sector employment by enterprise size, 1991**

Percentages

| | Enterprise size (number of persons employed) | | | |
	1-19	20-99	100-499	500+
Denmark[1]	**39.8**	**22.8**	**17.3**	**20.1**
Belgium	25.2	20.8	19.1	34.9
Finland[2,3]	26.3	18.0	17.0	38.6
France	29.1	21.0	16.2	33.7
Germany	25.9	18.7	18.2	37.2
Greece[4]	19.4	34.0	29.3	17.3
Italy[3]	54.0	15.0	11.3	19.7
Portugal	34.6	25.0	19.5	21.0
Spain	38.8	24.3	15.5	21.4
United Kingdom[2]	33.0	16.1	17.2	33.8

1. Private economy except extractive industries.
2. 0-19 instead of 1-19.
3. Figures relate to 1989.
4. 10-19 instead of 1-19.
Source: Eurostat.

Diagram 19. **LARGE SCALE ENTERPRISES**
1991

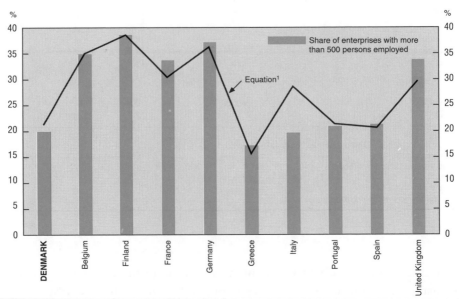

1. Equation = 10.13 + .013831* GDP (PPP, 1990) + .36822* Exports (% of GDP, 1990) + .5236* Dummy (Finland).
   T–values = 2.6   3.9   3.5   4.1
   R–squared = .8261, Adjusted R–squared = .7392.
Source: OECD, Eurostat.

62

during the first three years after they establish their own commercial company. Such firms appear to be rather vulnerable to bankruptcy, start-up companies as a whole standing only a 57 per cent chance of surviving five years.

A further characteristic is the relatively small dependence on foreign direct investment in Denmark (Diagram 20), albeit with a marked increase towards the end of the period, which – in the case of inward investment – partly reflects attempts of Swedish corporations to gain a foothold in the EC single market. While linked to the small size of most enterprises, low foreign direct investment raises the concern that Denmark's industrial development has been slow to take advantage of the international dispersion of technology and globalisation of industries. Most in- and outgoing investment relates to the service sector, with the financial sector the largest contributor to outgoing investment and the trade and services sector the main recipient of foreign investment.[13] Among manufacturing industries, the food and beverages sector has been most active in investing abroad.

Diagram 20. **RELATIVE GROSS DIRECT INVESTMENT**[1]
(ratio, OECD average = 1)

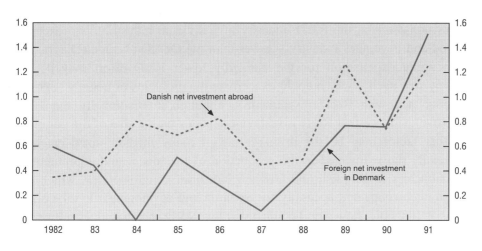

1. Danish investment as per cent of Danish value added relative to OECD investment as per cent of OECD value added.
Source: OECD, *International direct investment,* 1993.

Comparative advantage

Despite the relative smallness of Danish firms, the importance of scale-intensive sectors in both production and exports is among the highest in the OECD area (Diagram 21).[14] This finding appears to be attributable mainly to the relative importance of food and beverages, chemicals and shipbuilding, all of which are considered scale-intensive industries.[15] A further observation is that Danish industries are concentrated in sectors with a high degree of product differentiation (metal products, food and beverages). This may, in turn, be seen as a logical consequence of the combination of comparative advantages in scale-intense productions and limited average company size, encouraging industries to take up production of specialised "niche products" where the full benefits of scale can be reaped at a limited overall production level.

The standard separation of high- and low-tech industries focuses on average R&D intensity in individual sectors, such that the resulting definition mainly applies to total R&D content in terms of end-products. By such a standard the bulk of Danish industrial production is characterised as low-tech, since food and beverages, wood and paper products, metal products and – somewhat more controversially – shipbuilding fall in this category (Table 22). In addition to the compositional effect, the R&D intensity of individual industries is – except for the food and beverages industry – lower than the OECD average (Diagram 22). One possible explanation for the markedly lower R&D effort may be small company size itself – which could exacerbate the problems of negative externalities associated with R&D investment – although internationally there is no conclusive evidence that R&D investment depends on the size of the company.[16] A further factor may be the primary role of many medium-sized enterprises – especially those engaged in the production of machinery and equipment – as sub-contractors to Swedish and German industrial conglomerates, which could imply limited scope and necessity for research and development to take place in Denmark. It should, however, be noted that low R&D spending does not necessarily equate with poor R&D results. An examination of patent application data reveals that some Danish industries, such as machinery and equipment, show a comparatively low cost-per-patent ratio (measured as R&D spending per patent).[17]

Diagram 21. **MANUFACTURING SECTOR TECHNOLOGY AND MARKET STRUCTURE**[1]

Percentage points deviation from OECD average, 1981 to 1990

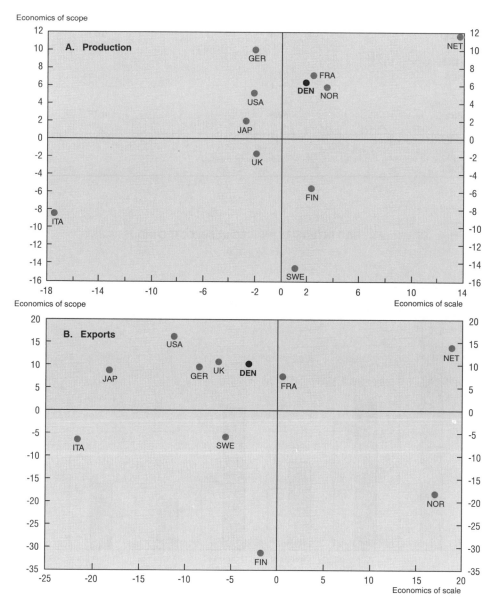

1. Share of manufacturing industry subject to economics of scale and economics of scope, respectively.
Source: OECD.

Table 22. **Technology and investment intensity**

In 1990

	Distribution of value added[1] per cent	Investment intensity[2]
High-technology[3]		
Denmark	**12.4**	**0.12**
World	20.0	0.08
Medium-technology[3]		
Denmark	**27.8**	**0.15**
World	30.1	0.10
Low-technology[3]		
Denmark	**59.8**	**0.15**
World	49.9	0.09

1. Share of total value added.
2. Gross investment divided by value added.
3. The division of industrial sectors by technology is described in Annex IV.
Source: OECD.

Diagram 22. **R&D INTENSITY INDICES IN SELECTED INDUSTRIES[1]**

(OECD = 100)

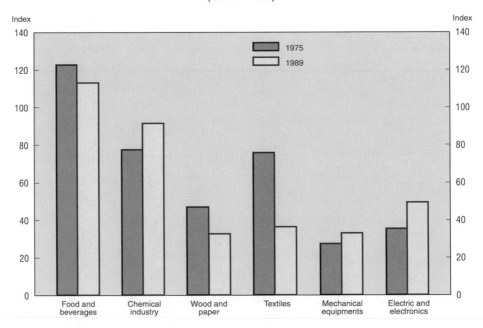

1. R&D spending relative to sectoral value added.
Source: OECD.

In any case, there is much less evidence that the production *process* in Danish industries is low-tech by international standards. Table 22 points to an investment/value added ratio across industries – with textiles as a notable exception – above the OECD-average. This suggests that new production technologies are rapidly implemented and employed in most industrial sectors.[18] Furthermore, data on patent applications point to a high degree of innovation in technical and thermal processes, which further underpins the observation of relatively high-tech Danish production processes.

Performance indicators

When assessing the economic performance of the business sector, the main criterion of success may be taken to be an ability to generate high value added on the basis of given resources. Employment-creation objectives are, in the longer run, best met through an optimal allocation of productive resources, and indicators such as export performance, productivity growth and profitability are all evidence of the dynamism needed to adapt the economy to the challenges posed by new technologies and competition from lower wage-cost economies. In the short-run, however, the process of resource reallocation may be very uneven, so that individual segments of the business sector – particularly in the sheltered service sector – may be slower to adapt to change than the internationally-exposed ones, and there may be large sectoral differences in performance.

Trends in employment and production

Over the last two decades the shift of resources from primary production and manufacturing industries towards the service sectors, which has been a feature of development of most OECD countries, has been relatively pronounced in Denmark (Diagram 23). Whereas the OECD on average registered an unchanged industrial employment over the period, Denmark recorded a decline of almost 20 per cent, most of which occurred during the mid-1970s. The increase in service sector employment, on the other hand, was in line with the rest of the OECD through the 1970s and 1980s – despite the fact that internationally high female participation rates already added to the service employment at the start of the period. However, the years of low growth since 1986 brought protracted decreases in service sector employment.

Diagram 23. **SECTORAL EMPLOYMENT TRENDS**

1970 = 100

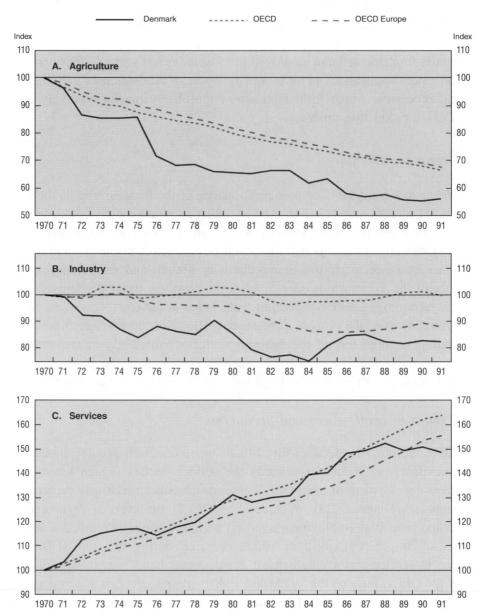

Source: OECD.

The sizeable drop in industrial employment during the 1970s was triggered by declines in industrial output, spurred mainly by a loss in international competitiveness, as Denmark maintained full wage indexation in the wake of the first oil crisis (Diagram 24). Losses in export market shares – as well as increased foreign penetration on the domestic market – led to a contraction in output and encouraged enterprises to improve competitiveness through labour shedding. Since 1980, the trend has been reversed with industrial output performing relatively well, but with labour productivity increasing even more than output so that there has been a net loss of jobs in the manufacturing sector.

Diagram 24. **MANUFACTURING VALUE ADDED
AND RELATIVE LABOUR COSTS[1]**

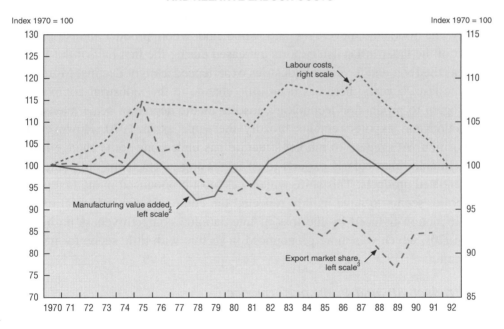

1. Denmark relative to the OECD.
2. Current prices.
3. Excluding agriculture.
Source: OECD.

69

Sectoral export performance

In terms of industrial sectors, the export performance of manufacturing industry during the latest decade has been uneven. While the average annual export growth of the manufacturing sector over the period 1982 to 1991 amounted to 8.6 per cent (in current prices), which was below the market growth of 9.7 per cent, three industrial sectors (wood, paper and chemicals) recorded clear market share gains (Diagram 25). There is, however, evidence that Danish exporters have performed relatively worse on markets where growth has been above the average, while gaining market shares on low-growth markets. Among the fast-growing markets, only the relatively insignificant paper and paper products industry gained market shares, whereas both the wood products and chemical industries fared well on slower growing international markets. However, since 1989 all industrial sectors have recorded gains in market shares.

Indicators of revealed comparative advantage for the main industry groups have changed only little during the last decade. Diagram 26 indicates that for the two sectors displaying export specialisation markedly above the OECD average, namely the food and beverages and wood and wood product industries, the weight of the latter in Danish exports increased during the first half of the 1980s, whereas the food and beverage industries experienced a slight decline. Moreover, over the last 20 years there has been little change to the industrial composition with regard to production technology, insofar as the degree of scale intensity in production and exports remains broadly the same as in 1970. However, the composition with regard to market structure has undergone some change in that production and particularly exports to an increasing extent focus on markets for differentiated products. This shift, which was most pronounced in the first part of the period, seems to have mainly reflected the contraction in industrial exports and production induced by the loss of international competitiveness during the early 1970s, which was more pronounced in sectors with little scope for individual pricing.

Productivity and profit performance

During the past two decades, the Danish business sector has recorded a total factor productivity growth slightly above the OECD average (Diagram 27). Whereas the manufacturing sector as a whole performed somewhat less well than average it was broadly in line with neighbouring economies such as Germany

70

Diagram 25. **EXPORT MARKET SHARES OF SELECTED INDUSTRIES**[1]

Index 1980 = 100

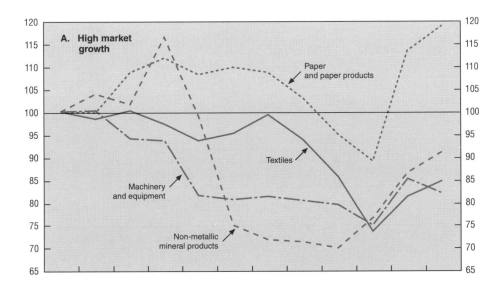

A. **High market growth**

Paper and paper products

Textiles

Machinery and equipment

Non-metallic mineral products

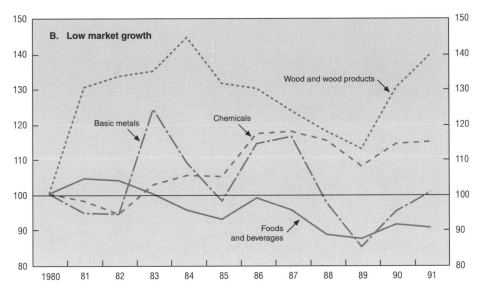

B. **Low market growth**

Wood and wood products

Basic metals

Chemicals

Foods and beverages

1. Current prices.
Source: OECD, *Foreign Trade Statistics.*

71

Diagram 26. **EXPORT SPECIALISATION**[1]
Relative to OECD

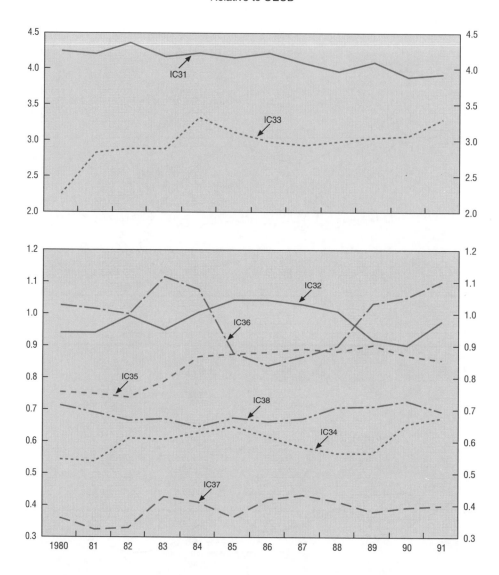

Note: Industrial classification codes for manufacturing: IC31 = foods and beverages, IC32 = textile,
   IC33 = wood and furniture, IC34 = paper and paper products, IC35 = chemicals, IC36 = non-metallic products,
   IC37 = basic metal industries, IC38 = machinery and equipments.
1. Each industry's share of Danish exports divided by its share of OECD exports.
Source: OECD.

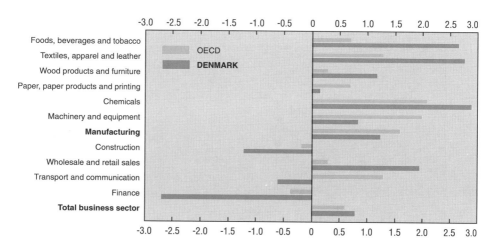

Diagram 27. **GROWTH IN TOTAL FACTOR PRODUCTIVITY, 1970-1990**[1]

1. Average annual growth.
Source: OECD.

and Sweden. However, the relative performance by sub-sector was far from typical for northern Europe in that factor productivity increases in the food and beverages, textiles and wood products industries were among the highest in the OECD – with increases in labour productivity being even higher – while that in the machinery and equipment industry rose somewhat less than average. Despite the sharp increases in productivity in the traditional "low-tech" sectors, wage shares remained broadly unchanged over the entire period, suggesting that the high rate of investment in new equipment aimed primarily to maintain profitability in the face of competitive pressure. In the service sectors, the financial sector performed markedly below average, mainly due to over-investment in the first half of the period when the sector was still subject to extensive regulation.

In many OECD countries the debate about the performance of the business sector usually emphasises the need for a strong presence in rapidly growing industries, arguing that rapidly developing products and markets offer the best opportunity for above-average returns. Examining this proposition for the OECD business sector as a whole, however, yields a result which is ambiguous (Dia-

Diagram 28. SECTORAL GROWTH AND PROFITABILITY, 1980-1991

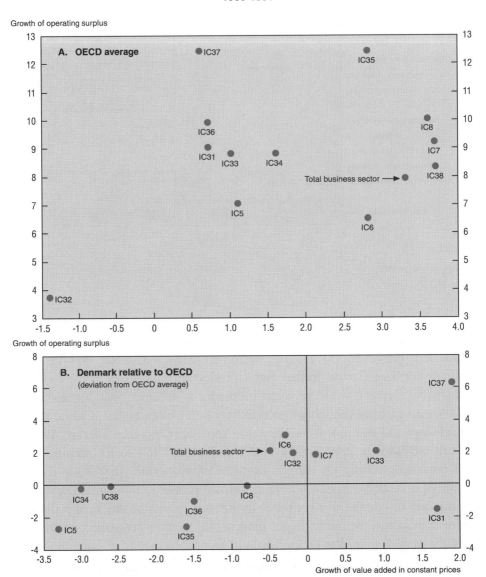

Growth of operating surplus

A. OECD average

Growth of operating surplus

B. Denmark relative to OECD
(deviation from OECD average)

Growth of value added in constant prices

Note: Industrial classification codes: *a)* manufacturing: IC31 = foods and beverages, IC32 = textile, IC33 = wood and furniture, IC34 = paper and paper products, IC35 = chemicals, IC36 = non-metallic products, IC37 = basic metal industries, IC 38 = machinery, *b)* others: IC5 = construction, IC6 = trade, IC7 = transport and commerce, IC8 = finance and insurance.
Source: OECD.

74

gram 28). The growth of nominal operating surplus does not seem positively related to the real growth in value added. On the contrary, among the fastest growing sectors only the chemical industry recorded a growth in operating surplus which was markedly above average. The implication is that in these sectors international rivalry in the promotion of "high-tech" activity can reduce profit margins. The rapidly growing machinery and equipment industry, which encompasses most of the high-tech sectors, showed a lower-than-average increase in earnings.

By comparison, the Danish business sector has performed rather well in terms of profitability (Diagram 28, panel B). The textile and wood products industries recorded an increase in operating surplus well above the OECD average, whereas the food and beverages industry – while recording a growth far above average – performed somewhat less well in terms of operating surplus.[19] Wholesale and retail sales and transport and communication industries, belonging to the fastest growing sectors in the OECD area, were among the best performers. But even sectors showing a markedly lower than average growth in value added, such as the paper and printing industry and the machinery and equipment industry, recorded increases in operating surplus close to the average. Overall, in the case of Denmark there thus does seem to be a certain positive correlation between the relative growth and profit performances. This may be connected with the tendency towards concentration in differentiated products and markets, allowing super-normal profits in the case of rapidly growing markets.

The role of policy: past experience

On balance, the above analysis indicates that the structure of the Danish business sector is relatively undistorted by subsidies and artificial incentives, with the result that the size-distribution and product-orientation of Danish industry for the most part reflect the natural characteristics and resources of the economy. If an industrial orientation toward low-tech products and a relatively weak national R&D effort has excluded Danish exporters from more rapidly growing segments of international trade, this needs to be set against the fact that returns have been relatively high in those sectors where Denmark has been successful. Moreover, rapidly growing labour productivity in a range of sectors due to high levels of investment has enabled industries to retain aggregate export-market shares in recent years. As in other European economies, a problem has existed with respect to the development of the private service sector, but this would seem to be a function of disincentives arising from high taxes on labour income and a compressed wage structure.

Competition policy background

Government ownership in incorporated companies other than public utilities is very limited in Denmark and, according to a guiding principle of Danish business sector policies, government is not directly involved in commercial activities. Most government holdings of equity in incorporated companies therefore relate to public utilities in the energy and transport sectors (Table 23). In telecommunications, the government has recently reduced its stake to 51 per cent in Tele Danmark, the national telephone company. Also, the stake in Copenhagen Airport has been brought down to 75 per cent and a partial privatisation of A/S EKR, which insures export risk, is planned.

Danish competition policies were treated in detail in the 1993 OECD *Survey of Denmark*, which identified an absence of competition in large segments of the government sector, with public enterprises being protected from the discipline of market forces through barriers to entry. Distortions and entry barriers were also identified in segments of construction, distribution and other private services.[20] In contrast to most other OECD countries, the Danish Competition Act, which came

Table 23. **Government shareholdings in incorporated companies**[1]

| Sector | Amount, DKr million | | Share of government share holding per cent |
	Total	of which: wholly-owned companies	
Energy	2 162	2 144	46
Transport	1 103	399	24
Telecommunications	890	237	19
Banking[2]	245	0	5
Industry and services	258	245	6
Total	4 659	3 024	100

1. Based on nominal value of stocks. Only companies with an equity capital exceeding DKr 1 million are included.
2. Includes only the partly privatised Giro post bank.
Source: Submission from the Ministry of Finance.

into force in 1990, does not impose direct limitations on collusive agreements or on mergers and acquisitions, but focuses instead on increased transparency, with anti-competitive practices registered by a public body entitled to disclose details of restrictive agreements concerning prices, discounts, bonuses and other matters of relevance for competitive conditions. Hence Danish competition law seeks to prevent the harmful effects of anti-competitive practices (the "abuse" principle) while achieving the benefits of concentration. Indeed, regulations have, in the past, been introduced to control entry or limit companies' operational freedom, where the outcome of unhindered competition is judged to be in conflict with efficiency objectives. Regulation is common, for example, in activities where economies of scale are thought to warrant only one producer.

Industrial support

Danish industrial policy has traditionally been largely non-interventionist. The relative level of subsidisation of manufacturing industries is, for example, among the lowest in Europe (Diagram 29) and – except for public transportation – virtually no direct support is given to the rest of the business sector. Most support measures focus on promoting the general conditions for business sector growth, via policies aimed at correcting market imperfections, or programmes aimed at infrastructure improvement and the promotion of research and development and risk-taking.

Direct support for industries

The overall amount of state aid to business, at around 1 per cent of GDP (Table 24), is rather small by international standards. Furthermore, in order to avoid uncontrolled spending and reduce the risk of industrial support schemes eventually being perceived as proprietary rights by the recipients, a large part of the industrial support schemes are assigned to "programmes" of limited duration, each subject to an annual general cash limit.[21] State support for investment (except for certain forms of energy investment), small and medium-sized enterprises and regional development is negligible, while support from the EC structural funds is limited. With virtually no coal and steel industry and a generally high GDP per capita across the country, Denmark only qualifies for regional support for economically depressed regions and structural adjustment in farming districts (Table 25).[22]

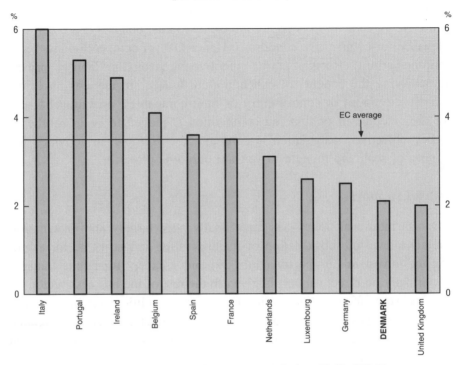

Diagram 29. **STATE SUPPORT TO MANUFACTURING IN EC COUNTRIES 1988-1990[1]**

(per cent of value added)

1. Excluding Greece. Greek state aid was estimated to 14.6 per cent of value added in 1988-90.
Source: EC Commission.

Subsidies to R&D and risk-taking

Support to the business sector has traditionally focused on measures to promote research and development efforts (R&D) and other kinds of risk-taking activity, such as exports to "high-risk countries". R&D support is generally associated with perceived market failures, connected with the disincentives for firms to undertake research where externalities prevent them reaping the full benefits of their research efforts or where company-specific research and development efforts are subject to economies of scale due to initial costs.

Table 24. **Central government support to the business sector, 1992**[1]

Support to	DKr million	Per cent of total
Specific sectors[2]	735	16.3
Research and development[3]	1 116	24.8
Investment	284	6.3
Small- and medium-sized enterprises	89	2.0
Regional aid	127	2.8
Export support	1 398	31.1
Shipbuilding[4]	749	16.7
Total, non transport	4 498	100.0
Public transport	3 484	
Total	7 982	
Memorandum items:		
Support as a share of GDP	0.9%	

1. Includes only government disbursements, except for shipbuilding support. Not including support to cultural activities, except for film-making.
2. Mainly support to tourism and distribution of newspapers.
3. Including R&D performed by government, targeted towards parts of the business sector.
4. Value of new orders multiplied by imputed subsidy rate.
Source: Ministry for Business Policy Co-ordination; Danmarks Statistik; Ministry for Industry.

Table 25. **EC support to the business sector**[1]

Annual averages

	EC support	Public co-financing[2]	Period
	DKr million		
Structural funds			
Support for economically-depressed regions[3]	28.9	38.9	1992-1993
Structural adjustment in farming districts[4]	41.5	50.7	1990-1993
Programmes			
Adjustment in regions hit by the closure of shipyards[5]	24.0	21.6[9]	1990-1993
Local iniatives in farming regions[6]	17.2	18.8	1992
Technological innovation in depressed industrial regions[7]	16.6	19.8[10]	1991
Co-operation in border regions[8]	36.4	39.6[10]	1991

1. Excluding measures aimed at agriculture and employment.
2. Also partly included in Tables 24 and 27.
3. Objective 2.
4. Objective 5*b*.
5. RENAVAL.
6. LEADER.
7. STRIDE.
8. INTERREG. Including infrastructure programmes not directly linked to the business sector.
9. Including loans by the EIB.
10. Estimate.
Source: Submission from the EC Commission.

Compared to other northern OECD countries, government R&D efforts are small, and thus do little to compensate for the relatively limited business sector R&D (Table 26). In addition, the share of government financing of business sector R&D is among the lowest in the OECD. Within this total the two main channels for assisting R&D in the business sector are general measures providing technological infrastructure and service and programme-related support to individual companies for initiatives in favoured fields. The government promotes R&D in small and medium-sized enterprises through a general network of "technological institutes", assisting companies with the development and implementation of new technologies. Among the activities covered by such programmes special attention is currently given to energy conservation, the environment, construction, material technologies and technologies related to food and beverages. Furthermore, the government has subsidised the creation of "industrial networks" to encourage enterprises to undertake joint projects.[23]

Table 26. **R&D spending by government and business, 1991**[1]

Per cent of GDP

	Government[2]	Business sector		Total
		Total	of which: financed by government	
Denmark	**0.69**	**1.00**[3]	**0.08**	**1.68**
France[4]	0.94	1.46	0.29	2.40
Germany	0.81	1.82	0.20	2.63
Netherlands[4]	0.84	1.14	0.14	1.98
Norway	0.83	1.00	0.19	1.83
Sweden[5]	1.01	1.81	0.21	2.83
United Kingdom	0.64	1.35	0.20	1.99
United States	0.74	1.87	0.53	2.61
Average	0.81	1.43	0.23	2.24

1. By performance sector.
2. Including higher education institutions.
3. An estimated DKr 125 million per year (0.02 per cent of GDP) is financed by EC programmes.
4. 1990.
5. 1989.
Source: OECD.

Overall, the measures providing general technological services address market imperfections deriving from the size and structure of Danish enterprises. However, some of the individual programmes target industrial sectors which could be expected to perform R&D efforts on a fully competitive basis. In order to avoid excessive deadweight losses, most schemes promoting risk-taking for R&D as well as exports involve the obligation to repay support in case of commercial success. However, since no repayment clause obliges successful participants to pay a fee equivalent to the default risk, government support to risk-taking is not self-financing and entails a clear element of direct subsidisation.

Export support measures mainly focus on government guarantees for credits to purchasers of Danish exports, advice and assistance from the foreign ministry to exporters and – in recent years – support to sale and investment in eastern Europe. Export guarantees and direct advice are available to all companies but are seen to be particularly useful to eliminate risk and increase market transparency for smaller enterprises and new exporters. However, until 1992 the scope of government export credit guarantees was somewhat wider, total guarantees covering around 20 per cent of total exports. In 1992, guarantees for perceived low-risk credits[24] were transferred to the actuarially based A/S EKR, scheduled to be privatised. Guarantees remaining with the government cover broadly one-third of the previous level.

Support to specific sectors

As noted, traditionally, Denmark has avoided subsidising selected industries[25] – a policy facilitated by an industrial structure including relatively few traditional industries, such as basic metal industries and car making. Support to individual companies – either for reasons of promoting growth or for restructuring troubled enterprises – is virtually excluded, the general argument being that competition between rival national companies should not be distorted.[26] This *laissez-faire* approach has been instrumental in avoiding the preservation of declining industries unable to maintain production without continuing public support. Shipbuilding is the only individual industry enjoying considerable direct government support. While the Danish government argues in favour of EC countries abandoning support to this sector, it continues to match the subsidies of other EC countries.[27]

An exception to the tradition of non-interventionism has been the strong political tradition in favour of measures aimed at improving the quality and – particularly in earlier years – the quantity of housing. This has exerted a stimulative impact on the size of the construction sector but is likely to have crowded out investment in other parts of the private sector. Until 1986, relatively generous tax-deductions on interest payments coupled with high marginal tax rates, secured a high and increasing demand for owner-occupied housing since the taxation of imputed rent of owner-occupied dwellings was relatively low. With the size of the population stagnating and the rate of home-ownership being among the highest in the OECD area, the tax-subsidies have been gradually scaled down, although tax concessions of limited importance on real estate investment by pension funds remain in place.

Remaining subsidies for owner-occupied housing mainly relate to improving the quality of the existing housing stock, and public authorities continue to grant direct support and interest rate subsidies to the construction of new council homes, dwellings in buildings owned on a partnership basis, youth apartments and homes for old persons. In 1992, 85 per cent of new dwellings started were subject to public subsidies. Grants for urban renewal have been increased in recent years, and – partly with job-creation in mind – direct subsidisation of repair and maintenance work in private homes has been introduced. Until recently households could obtain up to 50 per cent of the repair costs (up to a maximum of DKr 10 000 per project), provided they use registered companies. The rules have now been scaled down to 40 per cent of costs and a maximum of DKr 7 000. This scheme – which, due to its unexpected popularity, has had its funding stepped up from DKr 900 million in 1992 to DKr 2.5 billion in 1993 – gives rise to repair work worth six times the subsidy paid. Indeed, more than 20 per cent of the total production value of the construction sector receives public support, the figure rising to 40 per cent if civil engineering and business construction, which do not qualify for support, are excluded.[28]

Local authority support to industry

In contrast to the tradition of central government non-interventionism, local authorities have assumed a relatively active role in supporting various business sector activities, albeit at a limited overall budgetary cost. Generally, local authorities have focused on improving the general business conditions of the local areas *inter alia* through subsidising the staffing and activities of "business councils" – local committees of industrialists with political participation – and promoting special categories of business activity, among which tourism (Table 27). Furthermore, many local authorities are involved in training efforts targeted at the business sector and in promoting exports and contacts with the EC.

Local authorities have also participated in incorporated companies, although this has been largely limited to direct suppliers of goods and services for local authority use, such as energy producers and renovation, recycling and public transportation companies. For example, jointly owned enterprises provide local authorities with computer services and chemical waste processing. This has occasionally given rise to controversy, with private companies arguing that they could offer the same services at competitive prices and that publicly-owned companies have engaged in unauthorised sales of surplus production. Contracting of public work to private companies has recently gained in importance, although most local authorities are motivated by prospective budgetary savings rather than

Table 27. **Local authority support to the business sector** [1]

Counties	
Total outlays (DKr million)	130
of which:	
Tourism	26
Business councils	13
Municipalities	
Total outlays (DKr million)	300 [2]
of which:	
Business councils	85 [2]
Public transport [3]	1 455
Memorandum items:	
Persons employed [4]	408
of which:	
Counties	70
Municipalities	338

1. Counties: 1993; municipalities: 1992.
2. Estimate.
3. Both counties and municipalities. Figure covers 1992.
4. Including persons employed by business councils.
Source: Kommunernes Landsforening; Amtsrådsforeningen.

83

by "strategic" considerations. In the early 1990s local authorities contracted 15 to 25 per cent of their road construction, cleaning and renovation work to private companies.[29]

A new policy orientation

The largely non-interventionist industrial policy stance pursued thus far by Denmark would seem to have been important in allowing resources to be re-allocated in response to market forces, particularly foreign competition. Perhaps the single most evident area where social returns may be above measured returns is with respect to R&D where an increased emphasis on generic research might be appropriate in light of the modest spending compared with other countries.[30] The recent establishment of a Ministry for Business Policy Co-ordination,[31] however, indicates an increased interest in a wider and more active business sector strategy, defined rather broadly to include policies affecting infrastructure, market efficiency, education and private-public sector interaction. In the first annual report of the Ministry[32] a set of guidelines for future policies is defined, aimed at increasing support for the business sector environment or selected parts thereof where market imperfections can be demonstrated, or where economies of scale are perceived as giving scope for a degree of public assistance for developing new products and markets in sectors with a perceived growth potential.

Four areas are highlighted as offering a role for policy to improve the business environment:

a) providing a favourable environment for national "strongholds";
b) reducing strategic and financial barriers for small to medium-sized enterprises;
c) encouraging a public partnership with industry, while using public procurement to encourage companies to innovate and improve product "quality";
d) improving the general framework for suppliers of private services.

Support for national strongholds

A central element in the new strategy for the business sector is the identification of "strongholds"[33] – groups of industrial and service companies linked together through production technology, intra-industry trade or market orientation, which perform well in terms of value added, employment growth and exports compared with average domestic companies and comparable companies abroad. As a basic assumption, strongholds are built-up during long periods of time and maintained due to the accumulation of specific competences and knowledge in the companies involved. It is argued that a prerequisite for such an accumulation to gain momentum is a favourable general framework for the companies, consisting of good production factors, efficient markets, mutual competition and a beneficial interaction with other sectors, research institutions and the public authorities.

As a first step towards the naming of strongholds, an effort has been made to identify a number of coherent subsets of the business sector – so-called "resource fields". Each resource field can be characterised as a cluster of companies working in a similar general framework. It is thus within the individual resource field that one may expect to identify strongholds. The resource fields (Diagram 30) cover around 60 to 70 per cent of total Danish exports and private sector employment.[34] The Diagram indicates that traditional reliance on agricultural production and a – partly climatically founded – large consumption of housing services has given rise to two important resource fields. Furthermore, the Danish tradition in shipping and sea transports weighs heavily in the picture.

In identifying national strongholds, the main emphasis is placed on international performance. Gains in export market shares – preferably on markets characterised by rapid growth – and a high export coverage ratio are seen as essential. High value added – and thus indirectly high factor productivity – is a further indication of a stronghold position. Table 28, using relative wages as an indicator for sectoral earnings,[35] shows possible strongholds as indicated by a preliminary study by the Ministry for Business Policy Co-ordination.[36] Table 28 points to a feature of the business sector often described as a problem: many of the largest strongholds seem to be in sectors (food and beverages, transport/communication) with a slower than average international market growth. However, the table shows that many of these sectors can compensate for slower market growth through higher returns and a relatively rapid increase in market shares. Sectors with a clear indication of being strongholds (winning market shares and having either a net export or high earnings) make up for one third of total exports.

Diagram 30. **RESOURCE FIELDS**

Share of total export and private employment, 1990[1]

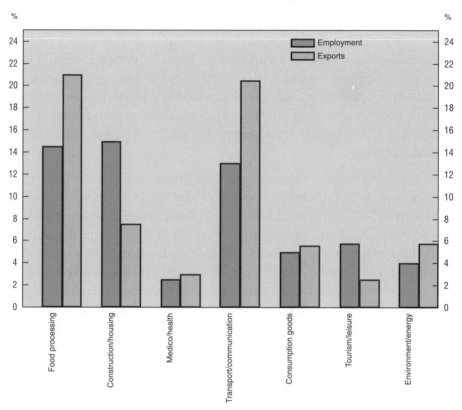

1. The resource field Business services is not included in the diagram.
Source: Ministry for Business Policy Co-ordination (1993).

The support to be offered to national strongholds, once identified, is intended to embrace enhanced public infrastructure provision (including education, research, transportation and communications), public/private sector liaison and government regulation. The Ministry for Business Policy Co-ordination (1993) states that national strongholds must be provided with general conditions which are at least as good as those of foreign competitors, but stops short of advocating matching foreign subsidies. The stronghold approach is thus likely to involve an increased emphasis on the public provision of higher-education and

Table 28. **Identifying strongholds**[1]

	Market growth relative to average[2]	Growth in market shares[2]	Export coverage ratio[3]	Relative wage level	Exports as share of total
Food and beverages					
Breweries	0.5	3.7	2.4	1.29	0.53
Fish	2.7	2.5	2.2	0.84	2.79
Soft cheese/milk powder	−0.8	10.4	10.8	1.12	1.28
Flour/pastry	−2.9	7.9	2.4	0.95	1.40
Sugar/chocolate	−6.9	4.3	1.8	0.99	0.94
Processed meat	−3.2	−0.3	10.5	1.07	8.11
Dairy products	−2.0	−2.9	9.4	1.10	2.57
Farming equipment	−3.4	0.9	0.9	0.80	0.87
Construction/housing					
Construction materials (metal)	2.0	1.1	0.8	0.88	1.58
Construction materials (others)	−3.0	2.6	1.1	0.95	0.94
Medico/health					
Pharmaceuticals	4.2	1.6	1.9	1.46	2.75
Transport/communications					
Sea transport	−3.1	4.2	2.9	1.11	6.79
Land transport	−1.2	1.0	0.9	0.93	7.25
Shipbuilding	−4.7	−2.1	1.2	0.97	2.11
Tourism/leisure					
Toys	3.9	−1.3	1.6	0.77	1.32
Consumption goods					
Household equipment	1.5	4.7	1.9	1.03	0.91
Wood furniture	2.7	5.3	5.3	0.77	2.30
Carpets/woven textiles	−4.5	2.0	0.6	1.01	1.06
Other					
Industrial machinery	1.3	1.4	1.1	0.99	2.53
Repro/printing	0.0	5.2	0.9	1.06	0.79
Paper/wallpaper	3.0	0.7	0.6	1.10	0.60
Measurement equipment	0.8	−1.1	1.1	1.02	2.53
Chassis factories	2.8	0.5	0.3	0.82	1.09
Chemical raw materials	−0.7	2.2	0.9	1.27	1.89
Tools/cutlery	−0.9	0.2	0.7	0.86	1.40

1. Figures relate to 1989 for the goods producing sectors and to 1988 for the service sectors.
2. Figures cover the period 1980 to 1991.
3. Export divided by imports (current prices).
Source: Ministry for Business Policy Co-ordination (1993).

communications facilities, as well as more extensive and direct public involvement in research and product development in the favoured areas.

Encouraging small and medium-sized enterprises

Although small companies have been among the most dynamic, various studies argue that barriers to growth exist as a result of scarce supply of venture capital, limited size of the domestic market and managerial problems in rapidly growing young companies.[37] The absence of a venture capital tradition, leading to relatively high cost of capital among newly established companies[38] is seen as one of the main factors discouraging entrepreneurship. To compensate, the cost of financing new activities in small and medium sized enterprises has recently been lowered through soft-loans from government-owned institutions[39] and guarantees to private financial institutions for up to 50 per cent of loans committed to new companies or activities. Financial institutions and pension funds have been invited to establish venture capital institutes which will be eligible for government guarantees of up to 50 per cent of capital committed to small and medium-sized enterprises. Under another scheme, new enterprises are offered a general subsidy for education and the purchase of business services (*e.g.* legal advice and accounting).

Public partnership with the business sector

The new strategy also sees a role for promoting innovation and growth by establishing a ''dialogue'' between government and industry: while small economies such as Denmark are considered to be at a disadvantage with respect to the modest number of larger corporations, this is seen as allowing the government to communicate more closely with such enterprises. As an adjunct to this policy, the aim is to encourage ''quality-conscious demand'', through public procurement policies. Public procurement policies are to be actively used to encourage companies to raise the quality of their products. The implementation of new technologies will be promoted through government development contracts, requiring public sector suppliers to develop new products and services for which a market in the private sector is perceived.[40] However, the amounts available for such contracts remain limited: in 1994, a modest disbursement of DKr 70 million is foreseen. Exporting sectors will be consulted regarding the composition of the assistance to LDCs to assure Danish companies a certain share of the associated production. Strategic contracting of public sector tasks will be undertaken to promote private sector activities in fields which can later be commercially exploited. The public sector also plans increasingly to enter into export joint ventures with private companies in fields where it possesses specific know-how. One such area is the Danish welfare system which may form the platform for exports of services such as kindergartens and old people's homes with both public and private participation (see below).

Local authorities remain a cornerstone in the public procurement policy, with special regard to joint export ventures and strategic contracting. Changes to the law allow local authorities to establish business promotion centres aimed at selected industries. They are now allowed to participate jointly in incorporated companies alongside commercial enterprises, subject only to the restrictions that equity may not exceed DKr 10 million per local authority and that the public shareholders may not exert dominant influence on joint companies. This enables local authorities to participate in areas where they possess special knowledge, and recent surveys show that 12 per cent of municipalities are already involved in such export joint-ventures with an additional 19 per cent expected to join shortly.[41] More than half the export projects so far relate to environmental technologies and a third to health and education services, most of which are aimed at markets in eastern Europe.

Developing tradeable services

A central aim of the new strategy is to improve the general business frame-work for suppliers of private services. Denmark already exports services corresponding to around 10 per cent of GDP, which is high even for an industrialised country. However, on the supply side important barriers to expansion can be identified:

- Insufficient use of competitive tenders in public procurement seem to have restrained growth possibilities in private service industries.
- Public providers of services may be at a competitive advantage due to the possibility of cross-subsidisation. Thus, rules about calculations of own costs must be precise to ensure that the granting of contracts are based on sound cost-benefit analysis.

On the demand side significant barriers are seen to arise from high VAT and marginal income tax rates which make excessive do-it-yourself work and participation in the informal economy very attractive. During the past 30 years these types of activity have become very common.

As far as the expansion of service exports is concerned, the expectation is that a number of service companies, related to the welfare system, will be able to expand their exports, partly in co-operation with the public sector. In the longer run, Danish exports are expected to shift away from basic industries and towards relatively knowledge-intense business services. Improving the interaction and co-ordination between the private and the public sector is seen as a key element here. Firstly, a great deal of knowledge of potential commercial value has accumulated in the public sector, especially in the welfare sector where Denmark has more experience with high quality services than many other countries.[42] This is a result of many years of great emphasis on providing services to all citizens in education, health care, infrastructure, etc.[43] The commercial potential of this knowledge are seen as best exploited if firms are established jointly by the two sectors. Similarly, private firms may be asked to tender for certain service functions in public institutions, especially in strategic areas where innovation is likely to ensue.

Domestically, private household services attract special attention. It is foreseen that future growth in consumption will lead to a further demand for welfare-related services which, in view of the already large size of the public sector, would have to be produced mainly in the private sector. Private home services (cleaning, gardening) are also seen as a crucial sector for job creation measures aimed at unskilled workers because the inherently low productivity in this sector leads to large employment gains for a given increase in demand. As a combined effect of high income taxes, VAT on all services and an even income distribution, the marginal tax-wedge when purchasing household services (interpreted as the number of hours a given person would have to work to purchase one hour of household services) ranged between 3 and 4 in 1993. To encourage the purchase of household services from registered companies, a subsidy of DKr 65 (US$10) per hour worked has been introduced and subsequently increased to DKr 85, reducing the tax-wedge to between 1.4 and 2 and lowering the price on household services towards the estimated level on the black labour market. To the extent that household services supplied under the subsidy scheme simply replace black market labour, the subsidy will tend to be fully financed through increases in income taxes and VAT. The subsidy may be combined with the "establishing grant" (see above) to unemployed persons, so that the overall effect is a strong incentive for unemployed unskilled workers to establish one-man companies in the household service sector.

Assessment

Available evidence supports the view that comparative advantage changes only gradually, and that sectors which have proven to be strongholds over a sustained period will tend to be so in the future. Thus, a strategy aimed at building on existing strengths and based on providing a favourable general framework for successful sectors should not be characterised as "picking winners". It may, however, if not carefully administered, introduce criteria for government assistance which are economically unsound. Concentration on fast-growing or R&D-intensive – rather than profitable – export sectors would be a case in point.[44] The overall performance of the Danish business sector should, by the structural and performance criteria outlined above, be considered as rather favourable. Following a period of reduced competitiveness in the 1970s, most industrial sectors have been able to restore profitability by means of internationally high levels of investment. High annual productivity increases have enabled perceived low-tech industries to remain competitive and among the main contributors to industrial value added. An internationally low level of industrial R&D investment has excluded Danish enterprises from participating in the production of a range of high-tech products with rapidly expanding markets, but there is no strong indication that such activities would have yielded higher than average returns.

Subsidised financing of small and medium-size enterprises gives rise to considerations about the degree of market imperfection in financial institutions' treatment of new enterprises. If, for example, the elevated interest rates banks charge to small and medium-sized enterprises reflect risk premia due to higher default risks, public soft-loans and other subsidisation are likely to lead to a misallocation of resources. Financial institutions argue that this is indeed the case, and industrial profit accounts for the latest five years show that enterprises with more than 500 employees record net profits (in per cent of turnover) which are almost twice the level of small and medium sized companies.[45] It may also be questioned whether the apparent lack of venture capital is primarily due to shortcomings in the financial system or in the tax system.[46] In many OECD countries private non-incorporated investors remain a major source of venture capital. In Denmark, high marginal taxation has discouraged household savings and directed them toward tax-deductible schemes – notably pensions savings.[47] Individually administered pension schemes are legally barred from investing in non-listed stocks, the ATP labour-market pension fundhas only recently been allowed to do so, and the Danish Banking Act sets limits to banks' investment in equity,[48] all of which has limited the venture capital available to new companies. Furthermore, institutional investors allowed to invest in unlisted stock have done so only to a limited extent, seemingly discouraged by the difficulty in disengaging from such investment. Encouraging these types of financial agents to enter the venture capital market via subsidiaries may thus be a feasible second best to addressing the problem of high marginal taxes.

Some controversy has also arisen over the issue of whether public partnership in commercial companies is beneficial, even when public authorities possess unique information. The policy of contracting public works to private enterprises is, indeed, a feasible way of improving the relation between cost and quality and of promoting private sector activity. Bids from local authorities should only be admitted if they participate in the bidding process through subsidiaries operated on a fully competitive basis (apart from contracts of negligible amounts). Plans to facilitate the procurement policy by placing the purchases of the entire public sector with one centralised body have been criticised for being disadvantageous to small suppliers and for extending monopsony power to the public purchaser.

As for the development of private services, the original subsidy of 65 kroner per hour turned out to be insufficient to trigger a sharp rise in demand, since during the first five months of 1994 the subsidy paid for the purchase of home services amounted to a mere DKr 20 million – 2 per cent of the cash limit for the year. Existing companies offering equivalent services to business typically charge prices of 160 to 170 kroner per hour, VAT included. Survey results indicate that household demand for home services at such prices will be rather limited, since only 2 to 7 per cent of all households are willing to pay prices in the order of 100 kroner per hour net-of-subsidies,[49] and they would not need to pay that much since ongoing rates on the black labour market are 50 to 60 kroner per hour. Even with the increase in subsidy to DKr 85 in June, only formerly unemployed persons establishing one-person companies under the government's "establishing aid" scheme are able to compete with prices in the black market.

V. Conclusions

The protracted weakness in domestic demand which had characterised the economy since 1987 gave way to a robust expansion during 1993, as the financial situation of households recovered from the disequilibria of the boom years of the 1980s. Despite the recession in Denmark's principal trading partners, and the associated weakness in export demand, GDP grew by 1.2 per cent for the year as whole. At the same time, the current account has remained in a large surplus and inflation has fallen to its lowest level for decades, with Denmark registering rates of wage and price increases well below the average for the OECD area. The most negative feature of recent performance has been the continued increase in unemployment.

With consumer and business confidence strengthening and resource constraints absent, the conditions for buoyant short-term growth seem now to be in place. The GDP growth rate is expected to rise to 4 per cent in 1994. Pent-up demand for consumer durables and the improved net wealth position of households should translate into a lower saving ratio, amplifying the effects of projected tax-induced increases in real incomes on household spending. Together with a recovery of external demand and lower international interest rates, this is likely to prompt businesses to expand capacity through investment in machinery and equipment. With output growing faster than productivity, employment is expected to expand for the first time since 1987, reversing the trend towards higher unemployment. Despite this, the slack in the labour market should suffice to prevent price pressures from emerging, leaving Denmark with continued low rates of inflation.

The unusually favourable overall conditions at the start of the recovery owe much to the maintenance of firm monetary conditions in recent years, imposed via the commitment to exchange rate stability within the ERM. This commitment came under pressure during repeated spells of turbulence in the foreign exchanges during late 1992 and 1993, as a result of which the authorities were called upon to intervene heavily to support the krone and to raise interest rates temporarily. Meeting the hard-currency objective required short-term rates to be higher than warranted by the recession in the latter half of 1992 and the first half of 1993. In the event, however, the successful defence of the krone and the cautious approach to interest rate reduction which followed the widening of the ERM intervention band in August 1993 have served to strengthen the credibility of the anti-inflation commitment, allowing an easing of monetary stance in step with falling German rates. The bond market was almost unaffected by the currency turmoil in 1992-93; long-term interest rates – which have a far greater impact on economic activity than short-term rates – fell steadily until early 1994, giving a strong impetus to growth. Recently, bond yields have firmed somewhat more than abroad, but in general developments in money and credit conditions have been supportive to activity, although real interest rates remain relatively high.

Meanwhile, following a period of budget consolidation, fiscal policy has been used to provide some support to activity, the Budgets for 1993 and especially 1994 embodying a temporary easing in fiscal stance. This policy shift has been motivated by continued disappointing increases in joblessness and should be seen in the context of a comparatively small structural budget deficit. However, the timing of these fiscal measures might give rise to some concern. The new Government, taking office in January 1993, was politically obliged to keep the budget already adopted, ruling out fiscal action in 1993. However, following the acceptance of the Maastricht Treaty in the May referendum, it was judged that financial market conditions were sufficiently stable to allow fiscal measures to be announced for 1994, as part of a comprehensive economic reform package. The acceptance vote and speedy parliamentary approval of the package appears to have led to a rapid improvement in consumer and business confidence, helping to stimulate recovery. Hence the bulk of the reflation will be concentrated in 1994, at a time when the economy will probably already have built up significant growth momentum, although the unemployment rate was still edging upwards in early spring. A moderately restrictive fiscal stance is planned for 1995.

The conjunction of fiscal and monetary policy easing means that demand may grow faster than implied by the projections. There is a risk that the households' saving ratio could fall more abruptly than allowed for, due to regained optimism and improved liquidity arising from an easing of mortgage-lending conditions, although the recent increase in long-term rates has reduced the probability of such an outcome. Moreover, while recent policy initiatives will serve to boost aggregate demand in 1994, some of the changes in labour market policy will tend to reduce the short-run productive potential of the economy. The new temporary paid-leave arrangements, available to the employed and unemployed alike, aim at a number of objectives, including improved education of the work force, job rotation and allowing parents more time with their children. While these measures are likely to reduce recorded unemployment in the short run and might to some extent prevent hysteresis, this could be at a cost in terms of reducing the availability of potential labour resources. These schemes have already proved to be much more popular than the authorities originally anticipated. If structural unemployment has increased over recent years, as some indicators suggest, resources might be put under excess pressure in the course of 1995.

There are several options for policy to forestall the danger of such an outcome, including the scaling back of paid-leave schemes and tightening of fiscal policy. Each of these options would appear attractive for structural policy reasons. The scaling back of paid leave schemes would increase labour supply, while further fiscal restraint would put government finances on a firmer debt-reduction course. As noted, a more restrictive fiscal stance is already planned for 1995, and according to their convergence programme recently presented to the EU, the Danish authorities are committed to eliminate the public sector deficit in the medium term. Reinforcing the case for fiscal action are doubts as to whether sufficient progress will be made towards achieving the more ambitious long-run goal of eliminating net public debt. On present medium-term budget policy assumptions, the budget will only move into structural balance if the structural unemployment rate does not exceed the official estimate of 8 to 9 per cent. A more restrictive fiscal stance would also be called for should there be any signs of overheating. Failing that, the burden of adjustment would fall unduly on monetary policy.

Reducing current high levels of public spending would also pave the way for reduction in the overall tax burden, further reducing distortions which are associated with government revenue raising. In this respect, the Danish Government is committed to keeping the rate of increase in public spending significantly below GDP growth, a policy implying a slow but steady reduction in the overall tax burden. Moreover, within the constraints dictated by the need to finance large government outlays, the current long-term revenue-neutral tax reform programme is already making progress in the removal of distortions:

- The shifting of the tax base towards pollutants and emission-generating activities should also reduce inefficiencies associated with negative externalities.
- The lowering of marginal taxes on labour income should also encourage people to seek employment, and the more uniform tax treatment of different types of income will reduce socially-inefficient tax arbitrage.

When the tax reform is fully implemented in 1998 the marginal tax rate on income for the average production worker will be reduced to about the 1992 OECD average. Even at this level, tax wedges will continue to reduce the dynamism of the economy and to reduce its job-generating capacity.

Recent changes in labour-market policy have modified the system in several areas. The possibility of renewing the entitlement to passive benefits by participation in activation programmes – which was criticised in the 1992/93 OECD Review of the Danish economy – has been abolished. Moreover, the decentralised administration of job offers and training schemes allows a better adaptation to individual and regional needs. Enhanced emphasis on timely training assistance to individuals at risk of very long-term unemployment and greater efforts to provide the very long-term unemployed with skills and labour-market experience should help to increase the employability of these groups. Although the devolution of operational decision-making to local labour-market boards should be useful in this respect, much will, however, depend on whether the authorities can provide the kind of training which genuinely increases job prospects for participants. Notwithstanding these reforms, replacement rates remain very high for low-wage earners, since the Danish government is not prepared to accept the social consequences of cutting benefits. Moreover, the duration of maximum combined ''passive'' and ''active'' support periods remains very long, and availability and willingness-to-work requirements have arguably become more difficult to enforce. While it is still too early to assess the impact of the new labour-market policies, these changes, including the paid-leave arrangements, would not appear to have provided sufficient foundations for a substantial reduction in structural unemployment.

While further reforms of labour-market policy may prove necessary for durable progress to be made in reducing unemployment, a vigorous and dynamic business sector is also a prerequisite for maximising income and employment growth. In this respect, the evidence presented in the Survey suggests that the Danish business sector has proved rather effective in channelling resources into relatively high income-generating activities. Factor productivity growth rates have compared favourably with neighbouring countries; scale-intensive manufacturing activities have been established despite the small size of the national market; and the preponderance of scope-intensive products in industry suggests an ability to take advantage of profit opportunities in specialised "niche" markets. While Danish products tend to be disproportionately represented in markets growing at a relatively slow rate, healthy profits have been generated due to the introduction of modern technology and resultant cost saving.

This favourable record has been achieved against the background of a non-interventionist policy stance, with market forces being allotted the major role of allocating resources within the private sector. Industrial support has been very low compared with other European Member countries, the exit of declining industries being, for the most part, unimpeded by government subsidies and initiatives to promote supposed "sun-rise" industries being notably absent. Although public regulations have impeded competition in some segments of the service sector, competition policy has sought to prevent excessive entry barriers from being erected by private agents. A strong commitment to an open trading system has also exposed domestic producers to the discipline of international competition.

Traditional government industrial support has been concentrated on areas where market failures may occur, such as R&D and export insurance. Public support to generic R&D would indeed seem to be called for, as problems of appropriability are likely to reduce research and development incentives for the individual firm. Nevertheless, care must be taken to ensure that public subsidies are channelled to "genuine" generic R&D activities. Subsidies to more specific projects invite the danger of dead-weight losses, with government funding replacing private funds without any effects on overall R&D effort. Public support in the form of export guarantees can also be justified by possible market failure, as long as such schemes do not go beyond correcting for the lack of private insurance.

Despite a relatively good business-sector performance, policies towards industry have recently been re-oriented towards a more activist stance. National "strongholds" have been identified, towards which more public resources are to be aimed, with the intention of strengthening the business environment. The creation and expansion of small companies, which is seen as being impeded by a lack of entrepreneurial spirit and enterprise capital, is to be facilitated by easing their access to equity markets. Product development is to be encouraged by government setting specific standards in public procurement, while co-operation between public and private bodies, partly in the form of joint-ownership of companies, is expected to expand service-sector export opportunities in areas where the public authorities have built up expertise.

This new more activist stance must be judged against two criteria: the presence of market failures and the ability of the authorities to correct such failures. In these respects, the national stronghold strategy clearly involves a degree of public involvement in activities where, by definition, the market has been very successful in determining Danish comparative advantage. The fact that there has been no deliberate promotion of high-tech industry in Denmark, for example, has probably been a factor behind the relatively high rates of return evident in those areas where industry currently specialises. Present strongholds have developed on their own, and there are doubts as to whether a policy oriented towards such sectors would have beneficial effects. In general, preferential treatment of certain activities, either "established" or new, carries the danger of misallocating resources.

There is little evidence of important capital-market failures which would justify subsidised financing of small and medium-sized enterprises. As a result, subsidised financing to such companies has been very low in Denmark, and is scheduled to remain so. High interest rate premia charged on this type of borrower reflects high default risks as much as excessive risk aversion on the part of lenders. On the other hand, the lack of a well-functioning venture capital market in Denmark may reflect disincentives due to high taxes, and the constraints imposed on financial institutions with regard to investment in non-listed companies. In this context, the planned easing of placement restrictions should increase the availability of venture capital. Possible market failures, such as asymmetric information between suppliers and users of funds, could still justify government subsidies in the venture capital market, but the need for such intervention should be assessed very carefully.

Closer co-operation between the public and private sector also risks distorting competition in the product market. Testing the cost efficiency of public service activities by allowing tenders from private producers has expanded the domain of market discipline, resulting in lower costs and a better allocation of resources in the economy. The coverage of the tendering process should be extended, since there is considerable scope for putting out service provision – particularly welfare services where entry costs are low – to the private sector. In this way, also, the private sector may be drawn into markets, domestic and foreign, with an important potential for employment expansion. To this end, tendering has to be subject to clear rules which ensure as wide a participation as possible, while public-sector producers need to be exposed to the same monitoring procedures and financial penalties in case of anti-competitive behaviour as their private sector counterparts. The use of public procurement to encourage product development in certain areas would seem to militate against such openness, insofar as specific product requirements could both limit the number of potential suppliers and extend the criteria for tendering beyond pure cost-benefit considerations. There are also doubts as to whether experiments with new products in the public sector are likely to identify future commercially-viable goods and services. Joint ventures between local authorities and private companies involve even greater risks of insufficient competition between public and private producers, as a result of which inefficiencies would need to be set against potential synergy gains.

In sum, having eliminated most of the imbalances built up in the 1980's, the Danish economy seems set for a period of expansion, based on monetary and exchange rate stability, relatively sound public finances and a favourable business climate. The least satisfactory feature is the high rate of structural unemployment, which may not be reduced significantly under current policies. The main danger is that, in adopting new policy initiatives to meet the unemployment challenge, measures may be taken that compromise the basis for steady long run growth, the most immediate risk being a return to a "stop-go" cycle. The Danish authorities have already determined that fiscal policy will move to a moderately restrictive stance in 1995, but should there be signs of overheating further fiscal restraint would be required. It is furthermore crucial that the ongoing reorientation of business sector policy builds on the competition-enhancing structural policy initiatives of recent years, so that business-sector energies are not diverted into rent-seeking activities. This would enhance potential growth prospects which, as long as these dangers can be avoided, appear to be rather promising.

Notes

1. See *e.g.* A.M. Christensen, 1987, Indkomst, Formue og Privatforbrug, *Working Paper*, Central Bank of Denmark.

2. The increase in the combined rate at the bottom of the income scale, due to the introduction of employees' contribution to labour-market funds, is unlikely to have much of an effect as very few workers will be affected.

3. The unemployed were entitled to two offers of participation in active programmes.

4. The combined maximum period of unemployment insurance benefits plus programme participation has been set at seven years (nine years if leave arrangements are taken into account). In the first four years (the first sub-period) the unemployed person has the right and duty to participate in an active programme for one year, starting not later than two years after entering into unemployment. In the remaining benefit period (the second sub-period) the aim is to keep the unemployed in ''active'' programmes to avoid marginalisation. To identify groups at risk and to better tailor programmes to individual needs, the labour office has to prepare an action plan for each individual out of work for more than three months.

5. Local authorities may provide supplements of up to DKr 35 thousand, but only within a ceiling of 80 per cent of previous wage.

6. The compensation level in the education leave scheme is 100 per cent of maximum benefits until 1 April 1995.

7. The method used to derive potential output is described in Annex II.

8. The output gap can be decomposed into 1) the deviation of actual output from normal output, the latter being determined by a production function using actually-employed resources, and 2) the gap between normal and potential output, which in turn depends on the gap between actual unemployment and NAWRU. In this framework actual output may exceed potential in the face of high cyclical unemployment if there is a large positive gap between actual and normal output.

9. The business sector is defined as the private sector less agriculture, fishing and extractive industries.

10. Oxelheim and Gärtner (1993).

11. Ministry for Business Policy Co-ordination (1993).

12. Even if the establishment rate in Denmark is rather low, it is not obvious that this would affect job creation. Davis *et al.* (1993) argue, based on various empirical studies, that once

corrections for changes in firm size over time are made there is little evidence that new jobs are created predominantly in new small enterprises.

13. 28 per cent of outward investment during the 1983-92 period related to the financial sector; 24 per cent of inward investment to trade and services.

14. The definitions used to classify industries according to production process, market structure and technological level are listed in Annex I.

15. For a discussion of the classification method, please see Martins (1993).

16. Based on recent empirical studies, Schmalensee and Willig (1989) argue against a relationship between size and R&D expenditure.

17. The data for 1989 – which is supported by findings earlier in the 1980s – show the following R&D costs (US$ millions per patent application).

	Denmark	OECD
Food and beverages	3.4	4.0
Chemicals	1.7	1.6
Machinery and non-electrical equipment	2.3	3.1
Electrical equipment and electronics	1.8	1.7

Source: European Patent Office.

Findings by Grilliches (1994) should, however, warn against too strong conclusions on the basis of patent data.

18. This finding is broadly supported by the Commission of the European Community (1990) which – regressing export coverage ratios on indicators of economics of scale and capital, labour and R&D intensities – concludes that Danish industries have a comparative advantage in capital-intensive production.

19. This may however be related to both the setting of input prices which is largely subject to EC regulation and the ownership structure which, in the case of meat processing and dairies, is dominated by the suppliers of inputs.

20. For example, concern has recently been expressed over regulations and pricing policies of pharmacies.

21. To increase transparency in the industrial support policy, the financing of support schemes has recently been adjusted, replacing most remaining measures, including tax deductions for certain activities and soft loans, by direct government outlays.

22. Two geographically-isolated counties qualify for EC assistance to economically-depressed regions. Further schemes relate to unemployment (objective 3 and 4) and adjustment of agricultural structures (objective 5a), but they are not directly related to the business sector. Furthermore, support under various programmes is given to local initiatives in farming regions, technological innovation in depressed industrial regions, co-operation in border regions and adjustment in regions hit by the closure of shipyards.

23. 2 000 to 2 500 companies are estimated to have been involved in such networks. Many of them were, however, linked to exports and marketing rather than R&D and diffusion of technology.

24. "Low-risk" credit broadly covers short-term positions with debtors in OECD countries.

25. One notable exception is occasional government preference for domestically-manufactured railway equipment.

26. Indeed, when in the mid-1980s Christian Rovsing A/S, the dominant actor in the Danish computer and micro-electronics industries, needed financial restructuring, the government preferred to let foreign competitors take over most of the company rather than to inject public funds.

27. Until the end of 1993, subsidisation relied mainly on financing shipbuilding through index-linked bonds with a maximum interest rate guaranteed by the government. In addition, individuals could obtain a relatively generous tax treatment by acquiring ships on a partner-ship basis. With effect from 1994, the old system has been replaced by a general subsidy of 9 per cent of the financing costs of new ships – equal to the upper limit on the level of subsidisation according to EC regulations. The new scheme entails an element of improved simplicity and transparency and will, according to government estimates, raise the total level of subsidisation by less than 1 percentage point when compared to recent years. However, new orders to Danish yards surged in late 1993 partly reflecting that the subsidy element in the old scheme was diminished by decreasing interest rates and inflation.

28. The part of total activity in the construction sector in 1992 which primarily took place due to public support is estimated as follows:

Urban renewal	DKr 2.6 billion
Repair and maintenance subsidy	DKr 5.0 billion
Subsidised new dwellings*	DKr 11.7 billion
Total	DKr 20.3 billion

* Calculated as the share of subsidised dwellings in total housing starts multiplied by investments in new housing.

29. Kommunernes Landsforening (1992a).

30. Hall (1993) and Cockburn and Grilliches (1989), based on sectoral data for industries in the United States, report social returns to R&D investment far above measured return in the performing industries.

31. The Ministry was merged with the Ministry of Industry in early 1994. The broad policy orientation, however, has not been affected.

32. Ministry for Business Policy Co-ordination (1993). The report lists a set of policy measures currently being implemented as well as longer-term strategies under consideration.

33. The "strongholds" are conceptually linked to the so-called "clusters" treated in detail by Porter (1990).

34. Ministry for Business Policy Co-ordination (1993) lists as an eighth resource area "business services", which has been left out here on grounds of a lack of homogeneity.

35. Using relative wages may pose a problem, since it disfavours sectors with a high proportion of either unskilled labour or companies located outside the major cities.

36. This study supports the findings of Kjølby and Larsen (1992), who, using specialisation indices in production and foreign trade, arrives at broadly the same strongholds.

37. For a discussion please see Maskell (1992) and Mandag Morgen (1993*b*).

38. Recent evidence suggests that small and new companies pay a premium of 1 to 2 percentage points above normal bank lending rates.

39. The overall importance of soft-loan schemes, however, remains limited. In 1993, subsidised lending amounted to around DKr 400 million – less than 0.05 per cent of GDP.

40. Porter (1990) quotes, as a successful example of such public procurement policies, the decision by the Danish government in the 1950s to provide free hearing aids to all persons with reduced hearing. This is seen as a main reason for present Danish dominance in the production of various sorts of medical equipment.

41. A detailed description is found in Den Kommunale Højskole i Danmark and Kommunernes Landsforening (1994).

42. However, Danish welfare services also tend to be comparatively expensive for the public purse, which may limit the prospective market.

43. An example of possible future professionalisation is hospitals. Only about half of the staff perform core medical activities. Many auxiliary functions such as catering, cleaning, administration and transportation can be carried out by private firms. Incentives to innovate in these functions will then be improved. The idea is that private firms should provide package solutions in specific areas such as ''cleaning and disinfection''. A firm responsible for such a whole area is likely to develop new ways of co-ordinating and organising the different functions. This is likely to lead to cost reductions and quality improvements, although the latter may be difficult to ascertain.

44. This risk is, however, acknowledged by the Ministry for Business Policy Co-ordination (1993).

45. This is, however, mainly due to higher gross financial earnings in large enterprises.

46. Relatively high capital asset taxation may discourage entrepreneurs from seeking stock-market listing of their company, since this usually entails an increase in the assessed personal wealth.

47. Another form of household saving which has enjoyed preferential treatment is the purchase of owner occupied homes.

48. Banks may not exert dominant influence on companies unrelated to the financial sector, except for temporary positions related to corporate restructuring.

49. Industriministeriet (1994).

Bibliography

Amtsrådsforeningen (1993), *Erhvervsfremme. Amternes organisering, funktioner og udgifter på området.*

Baily, M.N. (1993), "Competition, Regulation and Efficiency in Service Industries", *Brookings Papers: Microeconomics 2*, 1993.

Bechgaard, B., L.B. Kofoed and H.S. Mortensen (1993), *Evaluering af EF-programmerne RENAVAL og Mål 2 i Nordjylland.*

Boligministeriet (1993), *Bygge- og boligpolitisk oversigt 1992-1993.*

Christiansen, P.M. (1992), "Statslig erhvervsfremme – struktur, beslutninger, koordination", *Notat fra Industri- og Handelsstyrelsen*, December 1992.

Cockburn, I. and Z. Grilliches (1988), "Industry Effects and Appropriability Measures in the Stock Market's Valuation of R&D and Patents", *American Economic Review 78*, May.

Commission of the European Communities (1990), "The impact of the internal market by industrial sector: the challenge for the Member States", *European Economy – Social Europe*, special edition 1990.

Commission of the European Communities (1992), *Third Survey on State Aids in the European Community in the Manufacturing and Certain Other Sectors.*

Commission of the European Communities (1993a), "The economic and financial situation in Denmark", *European Economy*, No. 6, 1993.

Commission of the European Communities (1993b), "The European Community as a world trade partner", *European Economy*, No. 52, 1993.

Dalum, B. and G. Villumsen (1993), *Internal Specialisation and Trade Growth.*

Danmarks Nationalbank (1993). *Statens låntagning og gæld.*

Danish Government (1993), *Ny kurs mod bedre tider.*

Dansk Industri (1993), *Erhvervsfremme for teknologi, produkter, markeder.*

Davis, S.J., J. Haltiwanger and S. Schuh (1993), "Small Business and Job Creation: Dissecting the Myth and Reassessing the Facts", National Bureau of Economic Research, *Working Paper* No. 4492.

De af Folketinget Valgte Statsrevisorer (1991), *Beretning om EFs strukturfonde, II. Fondenes aktiviteter.*

Det Økonomiske Råd (1987), *Dansk Økonomi*, maj 1987.

Erhvervsfremmestyrelsen (1993a), *Medico/Sundhed – en erhvervsøkonomisk analyse.*

Erhvervsfremmestyrelsen (1993b), *Turisme/Fritid – en erhvervsøkonomisk analyse.*

Erhvervsfremmestyrelsen (1993c), *Transport/Kommunikation – en erhvervsøkonomisk analyse.*

Erhvervsfremmestyrelsen (1993d), *Fødevarer – en erhvervsøkonomisk analyse.*

Erhvervsfremmestyrelsen (1993e), *Bygge/bolig – en erhvervsøkonomisk analyse.*

Erhvervsfremmestyrelsen (1994a), *Forbrugsgoder – en erhvervsøkonomisk analyse.*

European Free Trade Association (1993), *Patterns of Production and Trade in the New Europe*, Geneva.

Finansministeriet (Ministry of Finance) (1992), *Finansredegørelse 92.*

Finansministeriet (Ministry of Finance) (1993), *Finansredegørelse 93.*

Finansministeriet (1994), *Grønne afgifter og erhvervene.*

Ford, R. and W. Suyker (1990), "Industrial Subsidies in the OECD Economies", *OECD Economic Studies*, No. 15.

Forsknings- og Teknologiministeriet (1993a), *Forsknings- og Teknologipolitik 93.*

Forsknings- og Teknologiministeriet (1993b), *Danish Research in Figures.*

Grilliches Z. (1994), "Productivity, R&D and the Data Constraint", *The American Economic Review*, March 1994.

Hall, B.H. (1993), "Industrial Research During the 1980s: Did the Rate of Return Fall?", *Brookings Papers: Microeconomics 2*, 1993.

Heum, P., P. Ylä-Anttila, P. Braunerhjelm and S. Thomsen (1993), "Firm Dynamics in a Nordic Perspective: large corporations and industrial transformation", *Working Paper* No. 401 from The Industrial Institute for Economic and Social Research.

Industriministeriet (1993a), *Redegørelse til Folketingets Erhvervsudvalg om kommuners og amtskommuners samarbejde med aktieselskaber m.v.*

Industriministeriet (1993b), *Notat fra arbejdsgruppen vedrørende pengeinstitutternes rolle i forbindelsen med finansiering mv. af nye og mindre virksomheder.*

Industriministeriet (1994), *Service til private husholdninger. Vækst i forbrugsserviceerhvervene i Danmark.*

Jacquemin, A. and A. Sapir (ed.) (1989), *The European Internal Market: Trade and Competition*, New York.

Kjølby, B. and L. Larsen (1992), "Dansk industris konkurrenceevne", *Samfundsøkonomen*, 1992 : 7.

Kommunernes Landsforening (1992a), *UDBUD – Stigende interesse og klar effekt.*

Kommunernes Landsforening (1992b), *Kommunernes erhvervspolitik. Kompetence, samvirke og ansvar.*

Mandag Morgen (1993a), *Hvad skal Danmerk leve af?*, part 1 and 2.

Mandag Morgen (1993b), *Barrierer for ny industriel vækst.*

Martins, J.O. (1993), Market Structure, International Trade and Relative Wages, *OECD Economics Department Working Papers*, No. 134.

Maskell, P. (1992), *Nyetableringer i industrien – og industristrukturens udvikling*, Copenhagen.

Ministeriet for erhvervspolitisk samordning (Ministry for Business Policy Co-ordination) (1993), *Erhvervsredegørelse 1993.*

Nellemann A/S (1993), *Evaluering af EF-programmerne på Lolland.*

OECD (1987), *Structural Adjustment and Economic Performance.*

OECD (1989), *Economies in Transition – Structural Adjustment in OECD Countries.*

OECD (1991), *Taxing Profits in a Global Economy.*

OECD (1992*a*), *Industrial Support Policies in OECD Countries 1986-1989.*

OECD (1992*b*), *Business Enterprise Expenditure on R&D in OECD Countries. Data at the Detailed Industry Level from 1973 to 1990.*

OECD (1993*a*), *Industrial Policy in OECD Countries: Annual Review 1993.*

OECD (1993*b*), *International Direct Investment Yearbook 1993.*

OECD (1993*c*), *OECD Economic Surveys – Denmark.*

Oxelheim, L. and R. Gärtner (1993), ''Small Country Manufacturing Industries in Transition – the Case of the Nordic Region'', *Working Paper* No. 394, Industriens Utredningsinstitut, Stockholm.

Porter, M.E. (1990), *The Competitive Advantage of Nations*, London.

Schmalensee, R. and R.D. Willig (eds.) (1989), *Handbook of Industrial Organisation*, Amsterdam.

Sundram, F. and M. Dam (1994), *Nye erhvervspolitiske perspektiver – rammer, konkurrenceevne, teori og praksis*, Institute of Economics, University of Copenhagen.

Sørensen, P.B. (1993), ''Beskatning, hjemmeproduktion, markedsproduktion og velfærd'', *Working Paper* No. 6–93, Institute of Economics, Copenhagen Business School.

Tyson, L.D. (1992), *Who's Bashing Whom? Trade Conflict in High-Technology Industries*, Washington DC.

Annex I

Supporting material to Part I

Table A.1. **Unemployment rates by selected unemployment-insurance funds**

	Insured persons 1991	Unemployment rate		
		1991	1992[1]	1993[1]
Self-employed	122 211	5.7	4.9	5.3
Academics	34 442	9.5	10.1	10.0
Public servants, etc.	128 909	7.7	7.9	8.1
Commercial and clerical workers	290 274	12.9	14.1	15.2
Bricklayers	10 254	25.2	24.7	25.5
Painters	9 636	14.0	15.9	17.7
Metalworkers	109 898	8.8	10.1	13.2
"Specialised" workers[2]	282 080	19.9	20.5	22.7
Female workers[2]	86 850	21.4	22.2	23.3
Garment workers	20 583	20.0	20.4	25.2
Plumbers, etc.	7 342	15.4	16.5	18.3
Graphic workers	22 448	12.6	14.5	16.8
Food industry workers	38 449	11.9	12.9	13.6
Wood industry workers	15 969	14.4	14.9	17.2
Joiners and carpenters	36 925	15.7	16.4	18.0
Restaurant and brewery workers	23 083	22.5	23.8	25.8
Engineers	39 949	7.3	8.4	9.5
Watchmen, etc.	27 525	10.3	11.0	12.1

1. The average of quarterly unemployment rates.
2. Mainly unskilled workers.
Source: Danmarks Statistik, *Statistisk Årbog 1992*; Danmarks Statistik, Statistiske Efterretninger, *Arbejdsmarked* (various issues).

Annex II

Potential output: estimation method

1.   Potential output estimates, used to calculate output gaps reported in Part III, are derived from a simple constant-returns Cobb-Douglas production function with labour-augmenting technical progress:

$$y = a \cdot (n + e) + (1 - a) \cdot k$$

where:

y = business sector value added in constant prices (in logs)
n = employment in the business sector (in logs)
k = capital stock (in logs)
e = "actual" labour efficiency index (in logs)
a = labour share parameter

This expression evaluated at trend labour efficiency, e^*, and at potential private-sector employment, n^*, gives the estimated potential output, y^*. The data used for the calculation come from the Analytical Data Base (ADB) in the Economics Department.

2.   The trend labour-efficiency index is derived from a crude measure of labour efficiency, which for a given labour share parameter – evaluated at the sample average – is given as:

$$e = (y - (1 - a) \cdot k - a \cdot n)/a$$

To purge this crude index of cyclical variations and of erratic variations in productivity and the intensity of factor utilisation the Hodrick-Prescott method has been used to smooth the series. The resulting series is taken to represent trend labour efficiency, e^*.

3.   The potential private sector employment is derived as the difference between the potential total effective labour force, *i.e.* actual labour force adjusted for structural unemployment, and public employment:

$$N^* = (1 - U^*) \cdot LF - EG$$

where:

N^* = potential employment in the business sector
U^* = NAWRU

LF = labour force

EG = actual public employment

The NAWRU is estimated by a linear interpolation of consecutive yearly observations on change in wage inflation and unemployment. For example, a deceleration of wages by about 2 percentage points at an unemployment rate of 7.7 per cent followed by an acceleration of wages by 0.5 percentage points at an unemployment rate of 7.1 per cent gives a ''raw'' NAWRU of 7.2 per cent. This series is smoothed using the Hodrick-Prescott filtre.

Annex III

Public sector debt

The size of Danish public sector debt is attracting increased attention, partly because of the currently rather sizeable public sector deficits, and partly due to concern over the ability to comply with the convergence criteria of the European Monetary Union (EMU). However, determining the size of government financial gross debt and assets is not straightforward, and becomes even more complex when attempts are made to account for future income and payments implicit in current legislation. This annex illustrates the wide range of debt figures currently in the discussion.[1]

Gross debt

Estimates of the overall burden of gross public debt (*i.e.* debt as per cent of GDP) in 1992 vary between 49 and 73 per cent (Table A2). The highest figure relates to general government debt as recorded in financial accounts which include debt incurred on behalf of publicly owned companies.

The debt definition used for the EMU convergence criteria[2] relates to gross debt of the consolidated general government sector. Thus, debt transactions between public authorities are consolidated (*e.g.* holdings of government bonds by the wholly state-owned Social Pension Fund and the local authorities) and public sector debt related to publicly-owned companies is subtracted. Furthermore, certain short-term liabilities *vis-à-vis* the public, such as trade credits, are excluded. The gross debt position in 1992 according to this generally applied definition is shown in Table A2 as version 1.

A second version, which is preferred by the Danish authorities, subtracts liquid central government assets from general-government gross debt. This version, shown as version 2 in Table A2, thus adjusts for the government financial position with the central bank and liquid assets, other than government bonds, held by the Social Pension Fund. The difference between the two different EMU definitions was equivalent to 14 per cent of GDP in 1992.

112

Table A.2. **Public sector gross debt, 1992**

DKr billion

	General government	EMU definition	
		Version 1	Version 2
Central government:			
Domestic	554	516[1]	516[1]
Foreign	105	105	105
Central bank			−31
Social Pension Fund:			
Government bonds	−44	−44	−44
Other assets			−89
Local authorities	82	82	82
Debt of public enterprises		−53	−53
Consolidation[2]	−72	−72	−72
Total	625	534	414
Total (per cent of GDP)	73.2	62.5	48.5

1. Excluding liabilities of tax authorities and public purchasers *vis-à-vis* the public.
2. Other than government bonds held by the Social Pension Fund.
Source: Danmarks Nationalbank (1993); Finansministeriet (1993); submission from the Ministry of Economic Affairs.

Table A.3. **Public sector net debt**

Dkr billion

	General government, 1992	General government, modified[1] 1991
Central government:		
Domestic	516	433
Foreign	105	90
Central bank	−31	−12
Lending to the public		−33
Social Pension Fund	−133	−105
Local authorities:		
Total debt	82	
of which:		
Long-term debt		31
Liquid securities	−11	−18
Consolidation[2]	−72	
Total	456	386
Total (per cent of GDP)	53.4	46.7

1. According to Finansministeriet (1993). Data are based on national accounts definitions.
2. Other than government bonds held by the Social Pension Fund.
Source: Danmarks Nationalbank (1993); Finansministeriet (1993); submission from the Ministry of Economic Affairs.

Net debt

The official definition of general government net debt is close to version 2 of the EMU gross debt figures mentioned above, the only difference being that liabilities related to publicly-owned enterprises are not included, whereas financial assets of local authorities are subtracted. (Table A3, first column). The Danish government (Finansredegørelse 93, 1993) has suggested a general government net debt definition including only the long-term debt of local authorities while not consolidating intra-public sector positions. In addition, 50 per cent of central government direct lending to the public is subtracted.[3]

The net debt figure still excludes important future income and outlay streams which are implicit in current legislation. The Ministry of Finance (Finansredegørelse 93, 1993) has recently attempted to evaluate the present value of the two most important concealed assets and liabilities:

- The unfunded "pay as you go" pension system for most public employees will increasingly burden future public finances.
- The deferral of tax payments, associated with the tax-deductibility for saving in private pension schemes, until the time of disbursement of the accrued pension.

Correcting the net debt figure for estimated present value of future income and outlays gives (1992, in per cent of GDP):

General government net debt	55
– deferred tax payments	35-40
+ public pensions	10
Corrected net debt	25-30

No attempt has been made to include present value of future social pensions on grounds the public pension system is not based on accumulated pension rights and future demographic trends are not fully known.

Notes

1. For a further discussion, please see Danmarks Nationalbank (1993) and Finansministeriet (1993).
2. Successful convergence is equivalent to reducing debt to 60 per cent of GDP.
3. The value of outstanding central government lending is estimated at 50 per cent of nominal value due to historically high default risks.

Annex IV

Industrial classifications

A. Production process and market structure[1]

Economics of scale:

  2 – Food, beverages and tobacco
  5 – Paper products and printing
  7 – Chemicals
  8 – Drugs and medicine
  9 – Petroleum products
  10 – Rubber and plastic
  13 – Iron and steel
  14 – Non-ferrous metals
  21 – Shipbuilding and repair
  22 – Motor vehicles
  23 – Aircraft
  24 – Other transport equipment

Differentiated market:

  2 – Food, beverages and tobacco
  7 – Chemicals
  8 – Drugs and medicines
  16 – Metal products
  17 – Non-electrical machinery
  18 – Office and computing machinery
  19 – Electrical machines
  20 – Radio, TV, communications
  22 – Motor vehicles
  23 – Aircraft
  24 – Other transport equipment
  25 – Professional goods

B. Technology based industry groups[2]

High technology:

3522	Drugs and medicines
383 – 3832	Electrical machines excluding communication equipment
3832	Radio, TV and communication equipment
3845	Aircraft
3850	Professional goods
3825	Office and computing equipment

Medium technology:

351 + 352 – 3522	Chemicals excluding drugs
355 + 356	Rubber and plastic products
372	Non-ferrous metals
382 – 3825	Non-electrical machinery
3842 + 3844 + 3849	Other transport equipment
3843	Motor vehicles
3900	Other manufacturing

Low technology industries:

3100	Food, beverages and tobacco
3200	Textiles, apparel and leather
3300	Wood products and furniture
3400	Paper products and printing
353 + 354	Petroleum refineries and product
3600	Non-metallic mineral products
3710	Iron and steel
3810	Metal products
3841	Shipbuilding and repairing

Notes

1. OECD STAN classification of industries.
2. International Standard Industrial Classification (ISIC Rev. 2).

Chronology of main economic events

1992

January

A new government circular requires state institutions to subject to market tests at regular intervals all activities where competition from external suppliers is feasible.

Experiments are initiated setting up multi-year contracts between the central administration and seven state institutions. The institutions are given more freedom of management but have to fulfil pre-negotiated requirements concerning productivity and quality advances.

March

The European Court of Justice declares that the labour market fee, which was levied on domestic sales from late 1987 to year-end 1991, was incompatible with EC rules. As a consequence of this ruling, the Government decides not to collect payment of the fee incurred in the last quarter 1991.

April

New rules concerning banks' liquid positions with the Central Bank come into effect, abolishing the automatic right of banks to draw on credit facilities, and limiting the option to place surplus liquidity in interest-bearing current accounts. Instead the Central Bank will issue 15-day certificates of deposits every week, and necessary liquidity to the banking system will be supplied through repurchase of such instruments or short-term Treasury bills.

May

The Government takes measures to stem the rise in unemployment. The measures, most of which were to be in effect only to year-end 1993, include: more timely offers of temporary jobs or education to welfare recipients aged 20 to 24, introduction of a job-rotation scheme, increased resources to subsidise child-care and care of the elderly by local authorities, and the establishment of more lightly-regulated and taxed business zones in areas particularly hard hit by unemployment.

The mortgage credit law is changed, making it possible for owner-occupiers to lengthen the maturity of old loans from 20 to 30 years and relaxing restrictions on lending by mortgage credit institutions for other purposes than housing.

Long-standing legislation to prevent local authority participation in business activities not considered of common interest to citizens is relaxed. The local authorities are granted access to participate in business activities in the form of guidance and co-ordination assistance, sale of knowledge aimed at ''system''-exports, and non-dominant capital engagements to the tune of DKr 10 million per local authority in private companies that commercialise local authority know-how.

June

The Maastricht treaty on European Union is rejected in a national referendum: 50.7 per cent of the voters against and 49.3 per cent for the treaty.

Parliament decides to reduce indirect taxes on beer and wine, effective from October 1992, and the diesel tax is increased to the minimum permissible level in the EC.

July

A committee on structural problems in the labour market (the ''Zeuthen'' committee) recommends changes in labour market policy, notably in the areas of the financing of unemployment compensation and the delivery of ''active'' labour-market policy.

December

The Government and the main opposition parties reach an agreement about the Budget for 1993, which incorporates a temporary relaxation of fiscal policy. Expenditures are set at DKr 351.3 billion (DKr 332.2 billion in 1992) and revenues are set at DKr 307.4 billion (DKr 293.9 billion in 1992). The main stimulatory measures include: increases in capital spending by the central government (1.5 billion); housing policy initiatives (1.1 billion); industrial policy initiatives toward small and medium-sized enterprises, shipbuilding and fisheries (0.4 billion); education and labour-market policy initiatives (0.4 billion). Measures taken outside the central government budget include an easing of borrowing restrictions on local authorities to encourage investment.

1993

January

The liberal-conservative minority government is replaced by a centre-left majority coalition government consisting of the Social Democratic Party, the Radical Liberal Party, the Center Democratic Party and the Christian People's Party.

February

The official discount rate is raised from 9.50 to 11.50 per cent and subsequently lowered to 10.50 per cent.

A two year wage contract for the manufacturing industries is concluded. The main elements are a gradual increase of minimum wages from DKr 66.00 to 69.70 per hour, continued wage payments during the first two weeks of illness and an increase in employers' contribution to labour market pensions.

A two year wage contract for the central government is concluded. The main elements are a gradual 1.5 per cent direct wage increase, increased employers' payments to the pension schemes and improved access to paid leave for education. A few weeks later, a similar contract for the local authorities is concluded.

March

The official discount rate is lowered from 10.50 to 9.50 per cent.

April

The official discount rate is lowered from 9.50 to 9.25 per cent.
Stamp duties connected with home purchases and consumer credits are abolished.

May

The official discount rate is lowered from 9.25 to 8.25 per cent.

The Maastricht treaty on European Union, including the Edinburgh agreements on Danish non-participation in stage three, is approved in a national referendum: 56.7 per cent of the voters for and 43.3 per cent against.

The government presents a blue-print for policies to stimulate employment and enhance the growth potential. The main elements are a labour-market reform and a temporarily underfinanced tax reform.

June

The official discount rate is lowered from 8.25 to 7.75 per cent.

Parliament approves a tax reform to be implemented gradually from 1994 to 1998. The main elements are: general reductions in personal income tax rates; introduction of payroll taxes; increased "green" taxes; broadening the business tax base.

Parliament approves a labour market reform effective from 1994. The main elements are: introduction of paid-leave schemes for child rearing, education and sabbatical purposes; limitation of the maximum duration of unemployment insurance benefits to seven years; increasing training and job-creation measures for the unemployed and the creation of more places in the education system.

July

The official discount rate is lowered from 7.75 to 7.25 per cent and subsequently raised to 9.25 per cent.

August

The exchange rate mechanism of the European Monetary System is temporarily changed. The bilateral fluctuation bands are changed from 2.25 per cent to 15 per cent.

September

The official discount rate is lowered from 9.25 to 8.25 per cent.

The government presents its Business Policy Report outlining initiatives to promote business sector performance. Among the measures under consideration are support to small- and medium-sized enterprises, subsidies for the purchase of household services and public sector partnership with parts of the business sector.

October

The official discount rate is lowered from 8.25 to 7.25 per cent.

November

The official discount rate is lowered from 7.25 to 6.50 per cent.

December

The official discount rate is lowered from 6.50 to 6.25 per cent.

The 1994 Fiscal Budget is approved by the Parliament. The expenditures are set at DKr 388.9 billion (DKr 362.3 billion in 1993) and the revenues at DKr 334.5 billion (DKr 310.6 billion), thus resulting in a budget deficit of DKr 54.4 billion (DKr 51.7 billion).

1994

January

The official discount rate is lowered from 6.25 to 5.75 per cent.

February

The official discount rate is lowered from 5.75 to 5.50 per cent.

STATISTICAL AND STRUCTURAL ANNEX

Selected background statistics

	Average 1984-93	1984	1985	1986	1987	1988	1989	1990	1991	1992	1993
A. Percentage changes from previous year at constant 1980 prices											
Private consumption	1.6	3.4	5.0	5.7	-1.5	-1.0	-0.4	0.0	1.0	0.7	2.6
Gross fixed capital formation	1.6	12.9	12.6	17.1	-3.8	-6.6	1.0	-1.7	-5.4	-8.2	-1.8
Residential	-1.5	20.3	-2.1	21.3	-3.2	-9.4	-8.9	-13.7	-11.8	-4.1	-3.1
Non-residential	2.5	10.5	17.7	15.9	-3.9	-5.8	3.9	1.3	-3.9	-9.0	-1.5
GDP	1.9	4.4	4.3	3.6	0.3	1.2	0.6	1.4	1.0	1.2	1.2
GDP price deflator	3.6	5.7	4.3	4.6	4.7	3.4	4.2	2.7	2.5	1.9	1.5
Industrial production	3.2	10.7	3.7	7.4	-3.1	1.9	2.5	0.1	2.8	2.8	2.8
Employment	0.3	1.7	2.5	2.6	0.9	-0.6	-0.6	-1.0	-1.8	-0.1	-0.5
Compensation of employees (current prices)	5.3	8.0	8.1	7.7	9.2	4.7	3.6	4.1	3.2	2.8	1.6
Productivity (GDP/employment)	1.6	2.6	1.7	1.0	-0.6	1.8	1.1	2.5	2.8	1.3	1.7
Unit labour costs (compensation/GDP)	3.3	3.5	3.6	4.0	8.9	3.5	3.0	2.6	2.2	1.6	0.4
B. Percentage ratios											
Gross fixed capital formation as % of GDP at constant prices	17.9	17.1	18.5	20.9	20.0	18.5	18.6	18.0	16.9	15.3	14.8
Stockbuilding as % of GDP at constant prices	0.1	1.2	1.0	0.6	-0.6	-0.1	0.6	0.0	-0.2	-0.0	-1.5
Foreign balance as % of GDP at constant prices	4.3	2.2	1.2	-1.1	1.4	3.6	3.7	5.9	7.4	9.1	9.8
Compensation of employees as % of GDP at current prices	54.6	54.2	53.8	53.5	55.6	55.6	55.0	55.0	54.8	54.6	54.0
Unemployment as % of total labour force	9.7	10.1	9.0	7.8	7.8	8.7	9.5	9.7	10.6	11.4	12.4
C. Other indicator											
Current balance (US$ billion)	-0.0	-1.6	-2.7	-4.5	-3.0	-1.2	-0.8	1.3	2.2	4.7	5.4

Source: Danmarks Statistik, Nyt Fra Danmarks Statistik; OECD, *National Accounts.*

Table A. **Supply and use of resources**

Kr million, current prices

	1985	1986	1987	1988	1989	1990	1991	1992	1993
Consumers' expenditure on goods and services	337 215	366 747	377 878	388 806	403 894	415 032	429 962	442 198	461 343
General government expenditure on goods and services	155 481	159 359	176 214	188 487	196 546	202 504	210 358	216 781	227 491
Gross fixed capital formation	115 192	138 370	138 033	132 226	138 953	139 357	135 976	129 424	129 835
Change in stocks	5 098	5 016	–5 075	–1 488	1 885	–917	–2 500	–100	–9 720
Domestic expenditure	612 986	669 492	687 050	708 031	741 278	755 976	773 796	788 303	808 949
Exports of goods and services (non-factor)	225 566	213 559	220 084	238 915	264 909	283 575	309 222	316 691	306 569
Imports of goods and services (non-factor)	223 480	216 555	207 226	214 892	238 936	240 442	255 639	251 013	238 663
Gross domestic product in purchasers' values[1]	615 072	666 496	699 908	732 054	767 251	799 109	827 379	853 981	876 855
Indirect taxes	112 913	130 880	135 974	139 551	140 201	141 523	144 888	149 114	150 984
Subsidies	18 358	20 060	22 011	25 340	26 955	28 354	28 740	33 484	31 962
Gross domestic product at factor cost[1]	520 517	555 676	585 945	617 843	654 005	685 940	711 231	738 351	757 833

1. Including repairs and maintenance.
Source: Danmarks Statistik, Statistiske Efterretninger, Nyt Fra Danmarks Statistik.

Table B. **Supply and use of resources**
Kr million, 1980 prices

	1985	1986	1987	1988	1989	1990	1991	1992	1993
Consumers' expenditure on goods and services	243 583	239 929	237 481	236 539	236 644	239 900	241 573	241 573	247 839
General government expenditure on goods and services	108 205	110 873	111 920	111 234	110 752	110 783	111 594	111 594	115 150
Gross fixed capital formation	91 276	88 703	82 808	83 639	82 179	77 777	71 409	71 409	70 138
Changes in stocks	2 506	−2 771	−603	2 559	139	−1 100	−100	−100	−7 008
Domestic expenditure	445 570	436 734	431 606	433 971	429 714	427 360	424 476	424 476	426 119
Exports of goods and services (non-factor)	154 454	162 295	174 922	182 193	194 833	209 922	217 679	217 679	214 044
Imports of goods and services (non-factor)	159 457	156 265	158 606	165 718	167 669	175 823	174 957	174 957	167 577
Gross domestic product in purchasers' values[1]	440 567	442 764	447 922	450 446	456 878	461 459	467 198	467 198	472 586

1. Including repairs and maintenance.
Source: Danmarks Statistic, Statistiske Efterretninger, Nyt Fra Danmarks Statistik.

Table C. General government expenditure and revenue
Kr billion

	1984	1985	1986	1987	1988	1989	1990	1991	1992
I. Expenditure									
Wages and salaries	104.8	110.3	114.4	125.8	136.3	142.2	146.8	152.4	157.2
Purchases of goods and services	49.6	53.7	54.9	61.1	64.0	67.0	69.6	75.0	76.3
Sales of goods and services	12.6	13.4	15.4	16.6	18.3	19.7	21.4	25.0	25.1
Consumption of fixed capital	4.3	4.9	5.4	6.0	6.4	7.0	7.5	7.9	8.4
Total consumption	146.1	155.5	159.3	176.2	188.5	196.5	202.5	210.4	216.8
Interest, etc.	54.1	60.6	58.7	57.7	58.3	57.5	58.5	61.1	58.6
Subsidies	18.6	18.4	20.1	22.0	25.3	27.0	28.4	28.7	33.5
Other transfers	107.0	112.6	117.8	129.0	144.3	158.6	164.6	178.4	188.3
Total transfers	179.7	191.6	196.6	208.7	227.9	243.0	251.5	268.2	280.4
Total current expenditure	325.8	347.1	355.9	384.9	416.4	439.6	454.0	478.5	497.1
Fixed investment	11.8	14.1	13.9	15.6	16.8	16.6	15.6	13.0	19.5
Change in stocks	-0.1	0.5	-0.7	-0.8	-0.8	-0.5	0.4	0.2	-0.5
Purchases of land and royalties, net	-0.8	-1.2	-2.4	-2.2	-2.4	-2.9	-3.2	-2.8	-2.5
Capital expenditure	10.9	13.4	10.8	12.6	13.6	13.2	12.8	10.3	16.5
Capital outlays for public enterprises	4.7	5.2	4.7	4.4	5.2	4.4	3.7	3.7	4.2
Other capital transfers	2.7	2.7	2.3	2.0	2.6	3.2	3.4	3.2	4.2
Total capital transfers	7.4	7.9	7.0	6.4	7.8	7.6	7.1	6.9	8.4
Total capital expenditure	18.3	21.3	17.8	18.9	21.5	20.8	19.9	17.2	24.9
Total current and capital expenditure	344.1	368.3	373.7	403.9	437.9	460.3	473.9	495.8	522.0
II. Revenue									
Surplus of public enterprises, etc.	6.8	6.8	7.4	4.5	6.0	9.1	6.1	5.4	11.2
Interest, etc.	21.2	22.9	24.5	26.4	27.6	28.3	31.7	31.7	34.2
Revenue from land and royalties	0.5	0.5	0.8	0.5	0.5	0.5	0.7	0.7	0.7
Indirect taxes	102.2	112.9	130.9	136.0	139.6	140.2	141.5	144.9	149.1
Direct taxes	155.2	175.7	195.5	208.9	226.2	235.4	233.3	244.8	256.3
Fees, fines, etc.	0.7	0.8	0.8	0.9	1.2	1.3	1.4	1.3	1.3
Obligatory social security contributions	10.4	11.4	10.3	13.3	9.8	10.5	11.9	12.2	13.2
Voluntary social security contributions	0.2	0.3	0.3	0.5	0.4	0.3	0.4	0.4	0.4
Imputed social security contributions	5.7	6.0	6.3	7.1	7.7	8.2	8.4	9.0	9.6
Other income transfers	10.6	10.1	11.9	13.7	14.0	12.6	13.7	14.1	13.8
Total current revenue	313.5	347.4	388.6	411.7	433.0	446.5	449.0	464.5	489.8
Gift and inheritance duties	1.1	1.4	1.7	2.2	2.1	2.1	2.2	2.1	2.3
Other capital receipts	6.4	7.1	6.1	6.8	7.1	7.7	10.7	12.1	9.6
Total capital revenue	7.5	8.5	7.8	9.0	9.2	9.7	12.9	14.2	12.0
Total current and capital revenue	321.0	355.9	396.4	420.7	442.2	456.2	461.8	478.7	501.8
Current surplus = gross saving	-8.0	5.4	38.0	32.8	23.0	14.0	2.5	-6.1	1.1
Current and capital surplus = net financial saving	-23.2	-12.4	22.7	16.9	4.3	-4.1	-12.1	-17.0	-20.2

Source: Danmarks Statistik, Statistiske Efterretninger.

127

Table D. Balance of payments
OECD basis
$ million

	1985	1986	1987	1988	1989	1990	1991	1992	1993
Exports, fob	16 984	21 268	25 657	27 498	28 696	35 944	36 717	40 596	37 311
Imports, fob	17 725	22 322	24 847	25 620	26 283	31 089	31 981	33 415	29 467
Trade balance	-741	-1 054	810	1 878	2 413	4 855	4 736	7 181	7 844
Services, net	-1 862	-3 156	-3 575	-2 982	-3 383	-3 121	-1 682	-1 492	-2 186
Balance on goods and services	-2 603	-4 210	-2 765	-1 104	-970	1 734	3 054	5 689	5 658
Private transfers, net	-53	-112	-55	-88	77	-46	-152	-132	-131
Public transfers, net	-66	-167	-153	-137	-221	-366	-717	-784	-183
Current balance	-2 722	-4 489	-2 973	-1 329	-1 114	1 322	2 185	4 773	5 344
Long-term capital (excluding special transactions)	4 319	3 025	8 110	2 404	-3 537	5 929	-1 674	4 488	18 943
Private	3 617	-1 304	5 594	3 928	-2 827	5 490	3 330	3 309	10 008
Official	702	4 329	2 516	-1 524	-710	439	-5 004	1 179	8 935
Basic balance	1 597	-1 464	5 137	1 075	-4 651	7 251	511	9 261	24 287
Non-monetary short-term capital	3	655	-727	128	-19	9	396	4 123	-4 243
Errors and omissions	-284	-276	94	-611	-339	-2 164	-2 249	-397	1 234
Balance on non-monetary transactions	1 316	-1 085	4 504	592	-5 009	5 096	-1 342	12 987	21 278
Private monetary institutions' short-term capital	303	-337	-760	745	1 208	-1 600	-1 525	-9 034	-21 696
Assets	-3 459	1 167	-4 230	-7 527	-4 290	-5 244	-2 610	-139	-15 201
Liabilities	3 762	-1 504	3 470	8 272	5 498	3 644	1 085	-8 895	-6 495
Balance on official settlements	1 619	-1 422	3 744	1 337	-3 801	3 496	-2 867	3 953	-418
Use of IMF credit	–	–	–	–	–	–	–	–	–
Special transactions	–	–	–	–	–	–	–	–	–
Miscellaneous official accounts	–	–	–	–	–	–	–	–	–
Allocations of SDRs	–	–	–	–	–	–	–	–	–
Change in reserves (+ = increase)	1 619	-1 422	3 744	1 337	-3 801	3 496	-2 867	3 953	-418
a) Gold	–	–	–	7	14	27	8	27	-33
b) Current assets	1 607	-1 366	3 738	1 245	-3 900	3 602	-2 934	3 931	-326
c) Reserve position in IMF	-7	-91	-4	149	26	-48	38	137	-51
d) Special Drawing Rights	21	33	9	-64	60	-86	19	-144	-6

Source: Balance of payments submission to OECD.

128

Table E. **Labour market and production** (cont'd on following page)

	Labour market						Industry				
	Number of insured	Registered unemployment				Unfilled vacancies [1]	Number of employed ('000s)			Monthly hours worked (wage earners) 1985 = 100	Volume of sales 1985 = 100
	'000 persons	'000 persons	Per cent of labour force				Total	Wage earners	Salary earners		
			Total	Men	Women						
1979	1 537.3	161.8	6.1	5.1	7.4	2 020	382.4	277.7	104.7	102	82
1980	1 630.2	183.8	7.0	6.5	7.6	864	374.8	268.4	106.4	99	82
1981	1 687.4	243.0	9.2	9.2	9.2	368	356.1	251.3	104.8	91	81
1982	1 774.5	262.8	9.8	9.7	10.0	208	354.8	250.0	104.8	91	84
1983	1 826.0	283.0	10.5	9.8	11.3	199	353.8	247.9	105.9	93	87
1984	1 871.7	276.0	10.1	8.8	11.7	400	372.0	261.9	110.1	97	96
1985	1 898.7	251.8	9.1	7.5	11.0	1 533	398.2	280.5	117.7	100	100
1986	1 920.9	220.4	7.9	6.1	10.0	1 836	408.1	284.7	123.4	104	107
1987	1 946.9	221.9	7.9	6.4	9.6	1 750	397.9	273.3	124.6	97	104
1988	1 981.3	243.9	8.7	7.2	10.3	1 180	385.9	263.0	122.9	93	106
1989	1 944.8	271.7	9.5	8.1	11.1	2 016	385.4	261.9	123.5	93	109
1990	1 957.6	271.7	9.7	8.4	11.3	3 366	386.4	261.9	124.5	92	109
1991	2 008.5	296.1	10.6	9.3	12.1	2 271	376.7	252.9	123.8	89	111
1992	2 138.1	318.3	11.4	10.0	12.9	1 583	369.2	246.7	122.5	87	113
1993	..	348.8	12.4	11.3	13.7	..	351.9	232.4	119.5	81	110

1. Average of monthly figures.
Source: Danmarks Statistik, Statistik Månedsoversigt and Statistik Tiårsoversigt.

Table E. **Labour market and production** *(cont'd)*

| | Building and construction, thousand m² | | | | | | | | Agriculture | Retail trade | | Passenger car registration |
| | Total | | Dwellings | | Industrial buildings | | Other industrial | | | | | |
	Starts	Under construction at end period	Starts	Under construction at end period	Starts	Under construction at end period	Starts	Under construction at end period	Output, production 1985 = 100	Volume of sales 1985 = 100	Value of sales 1985 = 100	
1980	7 760	9 441	2 789	2 760	3 395	4 429	1 577	2 253	96	94	65	73 961
1981	5 670	7 671	2 019	2 155	2 360	3 466	1 291	2 049	96	93	71	71 778
1982	5 341	6 544	1 750	1 726	2 532	3 141	1 059	1 677	96	95	78	85 512
1983	6 580	6 801	2 623	2 015	2 835	3 290	1 122	1 495	101	96	85	116 346
1984	7 889	7 556	2 981	2 073	3 522	3 860	1 389	1 623	100	98	93	134 475
1985	9 177	9 154	3 249	2 904	4 477	4 738	1 450	1 512	100	100	100	157 632
1986	10 425	10 493	3 563	3 352	5 500	5 761	1 362	1 381	103	103	106	169 492
1987	9 688	10 919	2 751	3 078	5 705	6 365	1 230	1 476	101	101	107	124 324
1988	8 525	9 749	2 389	2 784	4 958	5 669	1 179	1 296	99	100	110	88 770
1989	7 512	8 600	2 279	2 508	4 166	4 906	1 065	1 187	99	99	113	78 453
1990	6 610	7 220	1 673	1 774	4 044	4 424	891	1 022	101	100	115	80 837
1991	5 765	6 358	1 404	1 390	3 484	4 034	877	934	104	102	119	83 828
1992	5 414	5 711	1 383	1 266	3 137	3 593	897	852	109	101	120	84 170
1993	3 548	4 910	989	1 057	1 884	3 060	676	792	114	102	120	82 205

Source: Danmarks Statistik, Statistik Månedsoversigt.

Table F. Foreign trade, total and by area
$ million, monthly rates

	Total Imports cif	Total Exports fob	Imports by area						Exports by area					
			OECD countries			Non-OECD countries			OECD countries			Non-OECD countries		
			Total	EC	Other	CEEC	OPEC	Other	Total	EC	Other	CEEC	OPEC	Other
1978	1 234.5	990.6	1 047.8	628.2	419.6	50.9	39.6	96.2	819.6	484.4	335.2	26.9	48.0	96.1
1979	1 530.4	1 192.5	1 279.2	791.9	487.3	66.6	54.9	129.7	1 005.2	604.2	401.0	25.4	45.7	116.2
1980	1 610.5	1 369.8	1 339.2	808.9	530.3	72.5	51.6	147.2	1 151.2	707.7	443.5	26.9	56.9	134.8
1981	1 453.8	1 317.2	1 230.1	707.0	523.1	41.5	47.7	134.5	1 070.6	631.3	439.3	21.0	72.2	153.4
1982	1 397.6	1 250.2	1 168.2	699.8	468.4	46.9	46.9	135.6	1 028.9	624.5	404.4	18.5	66.7	136.1
1983	1 357.1	1 302.5	1 140.0	668.7	471.3	40.7	44.4	132.0	1 076.3	643.3	433.0	17.0	70.9	138.3
1984	1 378.3	1 298.3	1 143.3	662.1	481.2	52.4	44.7	137.9	1 072.4	586.0	486.4	22.0	60.4	143.5
1985	1 512.5	1 413.2	1 273.9	752.9	521.0	49.6	43.3	145.7	1 189.1	630.2	558.9	25.9	44.5	153.7
1986	1 906.5	1 774.5	1 652.7	992.3	660.4	45.3	30.3	178.2	1 512.3	829.3	683.0	33.1	46.4	182.7
1987	2 125.8	2 138.4	1 837.4	1 110.5	726.9	47.3	33.8	207.3	1 841.7	1 036.0	805.7	27.8	45.4	223.5
1988	2 161.7	2 261.5	1 868.5	1 117.7	750.8	45.7	37.7	209.8	1 952.0	1 131.2	820.8	35.2	48.7	225.6
1989	2 226.6	2 344.6	1 900.3	1 126.3	774.0	49.8	46.8	229.7	2 037.8	1 196.8	841.0	49.5	54.4	202.9
1990	2 647.6	2 927.7	2 289.7	1 382.8	906.9	64.2	37.5	256.2	2 534.5	1 528.4	1 006.1	70.1	60.8	262.3
1991	2 700.1	3 000.1	2 342.9	1 425.3	917.6	72.3	17.0	267.9	2 596.7	1 623.2	973.5	94.0	64.7	244.7
1992	2 800.9	3 298.1	2 428.6	1 497.5	931.0	88.6	15.3	268.4	2 830.2	1 795.8	1 034.5	95.3	69.6	303.0

Source: OECD, *Foreign Trade Statistics,* Series A.

131

Table G. Prices and wages

| | Consumer prices[1] | | | Net consumer prices (excl. indirect taxes)[2] | | Wholesale prices[1] | | | Building cost 1985 = 100 | Hourly earnings in manufacturing and construction (excluding overtime pay) kroner | | | |
| | | | | | | | | | | | | Unskilled | |
	Total	Goods and services (excl. rent)	Rent	Total (excl. rent)	Goods and services	Total	Domestic goods	Imported goods		Total	Skilled	Men	Women
1980	100.0	100	100	157.4	156.5	100	100	100	66	59.28	65.33	57.45	51.99
1981	111.7	109	108	175.3	176.3	115	113	118	74	64.52	70.77	62.87	56.69
1982	123.0	120	118	193.3	195.4	127	125	130	81	71.26	78.24	69.52	62.22
1983	131.5	131	130	205.2	206.1	134	132	136	89	75.98	83.14	74.24	66.71
1984	139.8	140	140	217.6	218.7	144	143	146	95	79.66	87.08	77.95	70.00
1985	146.4	148	147	227.7	228.9	148	147	150	100	83.42	91.55	81.61	72.82
1986	151.7	154	154	229.3	228.4	138	142	131	104	87.89	97.34	85.78	75.68
1987	157.8	160	161	236.5	234.8	138	144	128	109	96.25	106.79	94.02	82.50
1988	165.0	166	171	248.4	246.5	143	149	133	117	102.34	113.06	100.08	88.03
1989	172.9	172	182	261.4	259.3	152	158	142	123	106.46	117.39	104.13	92.23
1990	177.4	177	192	269.6	266.6	153	160	143	130	110.65	121.74	108.42	96.03
1991	181.7	180	201	276.7	272.9	155	162	143	135	115.26	125.75	112.94	100.36
1992	185.5	184	208	282.5	278.6	153	161	140	137	118.62	128.79	116.71	103.93
1993	187.8	188	214	286.5	282.0	152	160	139	140	:	:	:	:

1. 1980 = 100.
2. January 1975 = 100.
Source: Danmarks Statistik, Statistisk Månedsoversigt.

Table H. **Money and credit**

	Interest rates			Central Bank assets					Liquid assets			
	Annual average		End of year						Money supply		Bank liquidity [1]	
	Marginal rate on bank's borrowing at the Central Bank	Money market overnight rate	Average bond yield	Net official reserves (incl. gold and IMF reserve position)	Discounts and advances	Holdings of securities	Government accounts, net	Monetary base	M1	M3	Net liquidity position vis-à-vis the Central Bank	Net external
				Kr billion, end of period [2]								
1982	18.49	16.42	19.38	24.4	8.3	10.7	-9.3	14.2	86.6	172.3	-6.3	-2.8
1983	14.54	12.01	12.64	41.3	8.0	14.7	-22.5	15.4	108.5	217.4	-5.4	-7.0
1984	11.37	11.50	14.02	39.6	11.7	11.5	-16.7	16.4	122.1	259.2	-9.7	-7.4
1985	10.31	9.98	9.86	53.5	26.2	13.8	-21.3	17.6	147.6	306.4	1.0	-12.1
1986	9.09	9.10	11.61	35.9	42.9	23.9	-51.0	18.8	159.4	333.4	-34.6	-10.1
1987	9.90	9.87	11.73	64.4	18.2	24.2	-60.0	20.4	169.6	343.8	-17.7	-4.3
1988	8.74	8.32	9.78	76.2	1.7	26.9	-44.1	21.9	206.8	356.5	4.6	-8.0
1989	9.94	9.49	10.79	44.9	19.5	32.4	-34.5	23.1	210.9	367.9	-18.0	-13.4
1990	..	10.75	11.01	63.3	6.2	33.7	-38.4	23.6	226.4	391.0	-1.3	-1.5
1991	..	9.54	9.90	44.6	5.3	44.4	-16.0	24.2	248.9	379.4	14.4	7.8
1992	..	10.97	10.25	45.0	29.1	32.0	-35.1	25.0	243.5	374.6	-14.7	64.1
1993	..	12.10	7.74	69.8	81.7	38.2	-89.6	25.7	272.3	416.5	-46.8	200.5

1. Commercial and savings banks.
2. End-year figures, representing annual statement values, differ from end-December figures for 1989 which represent monthly statement values.
Source: Submission from Danmarks Nationalbank; Danmarks Nationalbank, *Monetary Review*.

Table H. **Money and credit** *(cont'd)*

| | Bank deposits | | Bank lending | | Circulating bonds (nominal value) | | | | Market for securities (market value) | | | | | |
| | | | | | | | | | | | | Increase in security holdings of: | | |
	From Residents	From Non-residents	To Residents	To Non-Residents	Total	Government bonds	Mortgage bonds	Other	Net supply of bonds (market value)	Net sales by Central Bank supply	Net supply on the market	Private banks	Private non-bank sector	Post Office giro, etc.[1]
	Kr billion, end of period								Kr billion, during period					
1982	..	..	..	..	610.8	204.0	379.0	27.8	59.2	–1.7	57.5	11.4	33.6	12.5
1983	..	..	..	..	724.4	272.5	417.5	34.4	86.9	–1.3	85.6	39.0	33.0	13.6
1984	..	..	..	..	837.6	331.3	468.3	38.0	84.7	1.5	86.2	17.3	53.9	15.0
1985	..	..	..	..	941.2	359.8	540.4	41.0	87.2	0.3	87.5	20.7	54.5	12.3
1986	379.5	33.1	351.3	33.1	1 003.5	351.1	608.7	43.7	54.4	–12.1	42.3	–7.4	33.0	16.7
1987	393.5	40.3	395.4	46.8	1 058.6	345.0	668.8	44.8	46.7	0.1	46.8	–33.7	67.8	12.7
1988	420.4	70.5	413.5	64.3	1 123.6	353.6	724.0	46.0	59.9	0.1	60.0	15.7	32.0	12.3
1989	423.9	91.9	445.1	80.7	1 163.6	375.8	739.3	48.5	31.1	0.3	31.4	10.5	9.3	11.6
1990	448.8	98.1	486.5	99.5	1 224.1	405.6	762.8	55.7	44.3	–2.0	42.3	–25.5	57.5	10.2
1991	460.4	55.5	491.8	99.1	1 315.4	462.0	790.3	63.1	77.1	–12.0	65.1	–0.3	56.2	9.2
1992	458.3	55.4	449.7	100.2	1 376.8	501.7	795.0	80.1	41.7	11.8	53.5	–11.0	62.5	1.9
1993	508.5	72.8	395.6	143.4	1 578.3	552.3	936.7	89.3	173.4	–6.9	166.5	–8.1	161.5	13.1

1. Including Social Pension Fund.
Source: Danmarks Nationalbank, *Monetary Review.*

Table I. **Labour market indicators**

	Peak[1]	Trough[1]	1980	1988	1989	1990	1991	1992
A. Evolution of unemployment								
Unemployment rate (register based)								
Total	1983: 10.4	1986: 7.9	7.0	8.7	9.5	9.7	10.6	11.4
Men	1983: 9.8	1986: 6.1	6.6	7.2	8.1	8.4	9.3	10.0
Women	1984: 11.7	1987: 9.6	7.6	10.3	11.1	11.3	12.1	12.9
Youth (age group 15-24 years)	1983: 14.3	1987: 8.3	10.3	9.0	10.2	10.2	10.1	10.7
Unemployment rate (survey based)			6.6	6.4	7.7	8.1	8.9	..
Number of persons experiencing unemployment (per cent of labour force)[2]			23.4	24.7	24.8	26.3	..	..
Average degree of unemployment for persons affected by unemployment, per cent[3]			30.1	34.6	36.8	36.9	38.9	40.0
B. Structural characteristics								
Participation rates, per cent[4]								
Total			81.0	83.8	83.4	84.1	83.8	84.2
Men			89.0	89.8	89.5	89.6	88.5	..
Women			70.0	77.6	77.3	78.4	78.9	..
Employment, per cent of population between 16 and 64 years			74.5	77.3	75.7	76.2	..	..
Self-employed, per cent of total employed			15.1	11.1	11.2	11.7	..	..
Part-time employed, per cent of total employed			23.2	23.7	..	23.3	23.1	..
Yearly working hours in manufacturing, per employee			1 650	1 615	1 596	1 596	..	..
Annual percentage change			0.6	0.1	-1.2	0.0	..	..

1. Most recent local annual maximum and minimum of unemployment rates, respectively.
2. Persons having received unemployment benefits.
3. Per cent of normal working time unemployed.
4. Survey based.
Source: Danmarks Statistic, Statistiske Efterretninger; Eurostat; OECD, Employment Outlook 1993.

135

Table J. **Public sector**

	1970	1980	1989	1990	1991	1992
Budget indicators: General government account						
(per cent of GDP)						
Current receipts	40.8	52.9	59.1	56.9	56.7	57.9
Non-interest expenditure	39.5	52.3	52.2	51.1	51.4	53.5
Primary budget balance	1.3	0.7	7.0	5.8	5.3	4.5
Net interest expenses	1.3	3.9	7.5	7.3	7.3	6.8
General government budget balance	0.0	-3.3	-0.5	-1.5	-2.0	-2.4
Structure of expenditure and taxation						
(per cent of GDP)						
Expenditure						
Economic category						
Income transfers (excluding interest payments)	10.8	18.4	20.7	20.5	21.4	21.9
Subsidies	2.7	3.2	3.5	3.5	3.4	3.9
Consumption	20.0	26.7	25.6	25.2	25.2	25.2
Gross investment	4.7	3.4	2.2	1.9	1.6	2.3
Functional category						
Education	7.1	8.2	7.2	7.1	7.0	7.0
Health	5.4	5.8	5.4	5.3	5.4	5.4
Social welfare	13.9	21.2	23.6	23.5	23.9	24.7
Housing	1.3	1.7	0.9	0.8	1.0	1.0
Economic services	6.0	6.1	6.0	6.0	5.5	6.3
Other (including interest payments)	9.1	13.9	16.9	16.2	16.7	16.3
Taxes						
Indirect taxes	17.1	18.6	18.3	17.6	17.4	17.3
Direct taxes	21.3	24.8	30.7	29.0	29.4	29.8
Capital taxes, compulsory fees, fines, etc.	0.3	0.4	0.4	0.4	0.4	0.4
Social security contributions	1.6	0.8	1.4	1.5	1.5	1.5
Total	40.3	45.6	50.8	48.6	48.6	49.1

	Before tax reform (1986)	After tax reform [1]	
		1987	1989
Tax rates (per cent)			
Personal income tax			
State income tax [2]			
Top marginal rate	45.1	40.0	40.0
Lowest marginal rate	19.9	22.0	22.0
Average rate	17.9	18.3	
Average local government tax rate	28.4	29.4	30.0
Average church tax rate	0.8	0.8	0.8
Maximum marginal income tax rate [3]	73.0	68.0	68.0
Wealth tax rate	2.2	2.2	1.5
Maximum combined marginal rate [4]	78.0	78.0	78.0
Income at which highest marginal State tax rate applies			
(per cent over average incomes [5] of skilled workers)	28.6	27.6	
Social security contributions of wage sum [6]			
Employers	1.4	2.1	2.5 [7]
Employees	2.0	2.0	
VAT rate	22.0	22.0	22.0
Corporate tax rate	50.0	50.0	50.0

1. Applied only to wage and transfer income.
2. Including contribution in 1986 to Old Age Pensions Fund and Sick-Day Benefit Fund.
3. Ceiling on marginal State and local government income tax rate.
4. Ceiling on marginal income and wealth tax rate (of taxable income).
5. Gross income minus interest expenses.
6. Including contributions to Labour Market Training Fund and Trainee Cost Refunding Scheme.
7. On VAT basis.
Source: Danmarks Statistiks, Skatter of afgifter, Oversigt 1991, and Statistike Tiårsoversigt 1991.

Table K. **Production structure and performance indicators** (cont'd on following page)

A. Production structure

	Share of private sector value added at factor cost						Share of private sector employment					
	1966	1973	1989	1990	1991	1992	1966	1973	1989	1990	1991	1992
Tradeables												
Agriculture	10.2	8.3	6.0	5.5	5.0	4.4	17.4	12.7	8.3	8.2	8.1	8.1
Mining and quarrying	0.2	0.1	1.2	1.3	1.2	1.1	0.2	0.1	0.1	0.1	0.1	0.1
Manufacturing	25.6	24.4	23.5	23.8	23.4	23.8	31.0	30.8	29.0	29.4	29.0	28.8
of which:												
Food, beverages and tobacco	5.6	5.4	4.9	5.0	4.8	4.8	6.1	5.7	5.1	5.1	5.1	4.9
Textile, wearing apparels and leather industries	2.6	1.9	1.1	1.1	1.1	1.2	4.6	3.5	2.0	2.0	1.8	1.8
Wood and wood products, including furniture	1.5	1.4	1.3	1.3	1.3	1.5	2.4	2.3	2.1	2.2	2.1	2.2
Paper and paper products, printing and publishing	2.8	2.6	2.6	2.5	2.5	2.5	3.0	2.0	3.0	2.9	2.9	2.8
Chemicals and chemicals petroleum, coal rubber and plastic products	2.2	2.5	3.1	3.3	3.4	3.5	2.0	2.3	2.7	2.8	2.8	2.9
Non-metallic mineral products except products of petroleum and coal	1.6	1.8	1.1	1.1	1.0	1.1	1.7	1.9	1.2	1.2	1.2	1.2
Basic metal industries	0.5	0.4	0.3	0.3	0.3	0.3	0.4	0.5	0.3	0.4	0.3	0.3
Fabricated metal products, machinery and equipment	8.3	7.9	8.6	8.6	8.4	8.3	10.1	11.0	11.9	12.1	12.0	11.9
Other manufacturing industries	0.4	0.4	0.6	0.6	0.6	0.7	0.7	0.6	0.7	0.7	0.8	0.7
Non-tradeables												
Electricity, gas and water	2.0	1.7	2.2	2.3	2.3	2.4	0.7	0.8	1.0	1.0	1.0	1.1
Construction	13.2	12.1	7.8	7.6	7.1	7.0	10.5	11.5	9.8	9.4	9.1	9.1
Wholesale and retail trade, restaurants and hotels	20.7	20.1	17.4	17.4	17.9	18.1	19.6	20.4	18.9	18.9	19.0	19.1
Transport, storage and communication	10.8	9.9	11.1	11.4	11.5	11.4	8.4	8.7	10.3	10.4	10.5	10.5
Finance, insurance, real estate and business services	11.2	17.5	24.3	24.3	25.1	24.3	5.4	8.0	14.7	14.6	14.8	14.7
Community, social and personal services	6.1	5.9	6.4	6.4	6.5	6.8	6.9	7.1	7.9	8.1	8.2	8.4
	As a share of total GDP						As a share of total employment					
Private sector	86.3	82.2	77.4	77.7	77.8	77.6	83.6	77.5	68.8	68.5	68.4	68.1
Public sector	12.9	17.2	22.0	21.7	21.5	21.7	13.2	21.0	30.1	30.4	30.4	30.8
Other producers	0.8	0.6	0.6	0.7	0.7	0.7	3.2	1.5	1.1	1.1	1.1	1.2

Table K. **Production structure and performance indicators** (*cont'd on following page*)

B. Sector performance

Constant prices

	Productivity growth (sector GDP/sector employment)					Investment — As a share of total industry investment					
	1987-88	1988-89	1989-90	1990-91	1991-92	1987	1988	1989	1990	1991	1992
Tradeables											
Agriculture	15.7	13.1	6.0	3.9	-4.1	4.5	4.1	5.1	5.8	5.0	5.5
Mining and quarrying	18.8	27.5	8.0	18.3	7.6	0.9	0.8	0.9	1.2	1.6	2.0
Manufacturing	3.9	2.3	-1.1	0.4	2.0	13.9	14.5	14.2	14.2	15.8	15.8
of which:											
Food, beverages and tobacco	6.5	1.2	4.6	1.0	4.7	2.7	3.1	..	..	..	..
Textile, wearing apparels and leather industries	-2.5	6.2	-4.9	4.3	-1.4	0.6	0.6	..	..	..	..
Wood and wood products, including furniture	2.1	-0.7	-2.9	-1.8	7.1	0.7	0.7	..	..	..	..
Paper and paper products, printing and publishing	-5.0	-0.9	-0.5	-2.0	4.9	1.6	1.6	..	..	..	..
Chemicals and chemicals petroleum, coal rubber and plastic products	0.6	1.9	1.2	-5.1	3.9	2.2	2.4	..	..	..	..
Non-metallic mineral products except products of petroleum and coal	-7.4	9.0	-1.5	13.1	19.3	1.2	1.2	..	..	..	..
Basic metal industries	23.6	23.1	-5.7	11.0	-5.1	0.1	0.1	..	..	..	..
Fabricated metal products, machinery and equipment	6.8	2.5	-4.4	-1.0	-4.5	4.4	4.4	..	..	..	..
Other manufacturing industries	14.5	4.7	-6.1	14.7	14.8	0.4	0.3	..	..	..	..
Non-tradeables											
Electricity, gas and water	3.8	-6.6	10.2	-9.3	16.5	5.5	6.0	6.3	6.7	5.5	6.2
Construction	-4.6	-0.9	-0.3	-9.4	-5.4	3.0	2.8	2.6	2.7	2.6	2.9
Wholesale and retail trade, restaurants and hotels	0.4	-2.5	5.2	6.3	2.1	6.1	6.8	..	..	..	..
Transports, storage and communication	4.9	7.5	11.0	3.7	8.8	13.3	14.9	..	..	..	..
Finance, insurance, real estate and business services	-1.3	3.7	2.8	-2.3	-1.0	26.3	26.3	..	..	..	..
of which:											
Dwellings	1.9	3.6	6.4	6.9	-2.0	23.5	22.9	20.7	18.2	17.0	17.7
Community, social and personnal services	3.6	-2.3	0.9	6.4	0.7	0.9	1.1	..	..	..	..
Others[1]						14.5	10.3	..	..	..	..
						As a share of total investment					
Private sector	2.7	3.3	3.3	2.0	1.7	90.0	87.6	88.4	89.1	88.8	86.5
Public sector	1.3	-1.9	0.2	0.6	-0.3	10.0	12.4	11.6	10.9	11.2	13.5

1. Investment in certain private service sector are poorly covered by basic statistics and have been grouped together in this sector.

Table K. **Production structure and performance indicators** *(cont'd)*

C. Other indicators

Per cent of total

	Number of enterprises			Number of employees		
	1980	1987	1988	1980	1987	1988
Size distribution of manufacturing enterprises Number of employees:						
6-19	49.4	48.4	48.7	9.6	10.2	10.4
20-49	27.3	28.9	28.8	14.5	16.3	16.7
50-99	11.5	11.8	11.7	13.8	15.0	15.2
100-499	10.3	9.7	9.5	35.1	36.3	35.2
500 and more	1.4	1.2	1.3	26.9	22.2	22.5
	1983	1984	1985	1986	1987	1988
Total R&D expenditure, per cent of manufacturing output	3.8	3.8	4.0	4.3	4.7	..

Source: Danmarks Statistik, Tiårsoversigt 1990, Nationalregnskabsstatistik; OECD, *Main Science and Technology Indicators.*

BASIC STATISTICS:

INTERNATIONAL COMPARISONS

	Units	Reference period[1]	Australia	Austria
Population				
Total	Thousands	1991	17 292	7 823
Inhabitants per sq. km	Number	1991	2	93
Net average annual increase over previous 10 years	%	1991	1.5	0.3
Employment				
Total civilian employment (TCE)[2]	Thousands	1991	7 705	3 482
Of which: Agriculture	% of TCE		5.5	7.4
Industry	% of TCE		24.2	36.9
Services	% of TCE		70.4	55.8
Gross domestic product (GDP)				
At current prices and current exchange rates	Bill. US$	1991	297.4	164.7
Per capita	US$		17 200	21 048
At current prices using current PPP's[3]	Bill. US$	1991	280	135.6
Per capita	US$		16 195	17 329
Average annual volume growth over previous 5 years	%	1991	2.8	3.3
Gross fixed capital formation (GFCF)	% of GDP	1991	20.5	25.1
Of which: Machinery and equipment	% of GDP		8.8	10.4
Residential construction	% of GDP		4.6	4.6
Average annual volume growth over previous 5 years	%	1991	0.3	5.2
Gross saving ratio[4]	% of GDP	1991	17.2	25.6
General government				
Current expenditure on goods and services	% of GDP	1991	18.3	18.2
Current disbursements[5]	% of GDP	1991	36.6	45.7
Current receipts	% of GDP	1991	33.7	47.2
Net official development assistance	% of GDP	1991	0.35	0.33
Indicators of living standards				
Private consumption per capita using current PPP's[3]	US$	1991	9 827	9 591
Passenger cars, per 1 000 inhabitants	Number	1990	430	382
Telephones, per 1 000 inhabitants	Number	1990	448 (89)	589
Television sets, per 1 000 inhabitants	Number	1989	484	475
Doctors, per 1 000 inhabitants	Number	1991	2	2.1
Infant mortality per 1 000 live births	Number	1991	7.1	7.4
Wages and prices (average annual increase over previous 5 years)				
Wages (earnings or rates according to availability)	%	1991	5.4	5.2
Consumer prices	%	1991	6.7	2.5
Foreign trade				
Exports of goods, fob*	Mill. US$	1991	39 764	40 985
As % of GDP	%		13.4	24.9
Average annual increase over previous 5 years	%		13.2	12.8
Imports of goods, cif*	Mill. US$	1991	38 844	48 914
As % of GDP	%		13.1	29.7
Average annual increase over previous 5 years	%		10.1	13.7
Total official reserves[6]	Mill. SDR's	1991	11 432	6 591
As ratio of average monthly imports of goods	Ratio		3.5	1.6

* At current prices and exchange rates.
1. Unless otherwise stated.
2. According to the definitions used in OECD *Labour Force Statistics*.
3. PPP's = Purchasing Power Parities.
4. Gross saving = Gross national disposable income minus private and government consumption.
5. Current disbursements = Current expenditure on goods and services plus current transfers and payments of property income.
6. Gold included in reserves is valued at 35 SDR's per ounce. End of year.
7. Including Luxembourg.

	Belgium	Canada	Denmark	Finland	France	Germany	Greece	Iceland	Ireland
	005	27 000	5 154	5 029	57 050	63 889	10 269	258	3 524
	328	3	120	15	104	257	78	3	50
	0.2	1	0.1	0.5	0.5	0.4	0.5	1.1	0.2
	735	12 340	2 612	2 330	21 782	28 533	3 768	140	1 113
	2.6	4.5	5.7	8.5	5.8	3.4	22.6	10.7	13.8
	28.1	23.2	27.7	29.2	29.5	39.2	27.5	26.4	28.9
	69.3	72.3	66.6	62.3	64.8	57.4	50	62.9	57.2
	96.9	583.7	130.3	121.2	1 195.8	1 587.8	70.2	6.5	43.4
	677	21 617	25 277	24 097	20 961	24 852	6 840	25 232	12 324
	71.5	520.6	90.7	77.8	1 035.6	1 257.8	79.4	4.5	40.5
	145	19 281	17 603	15 480	18 152	19 687	7 729	17 442	11 480
	3.2	1.9	1.1	1.4	2.7	3.8	1.9	2	5.4
	19.8	20	16.9	22.4	20.9	21.4	18.6	18.9	17.1
	10.4 (90)	6.4	8.5	7.4	9.4	10	7.8	6	7.7
	4.2	6.2	3.2	6.1	5.1	5.7	4.4	4.1	4.1
	8.5	4.2	–2.9	0.1	4.6	5.4	3.5	2.6	3
	21.4	14.4	17.9	14.7	20.7	23.1	15.3	14.4	23.7
	14.7	21.3	25.1	24.4	18.3	17.7	19.9	20	16.3
	54.6	47.9	57.2	46	47	44.2	47.6	32.5	49.9 (8
	49.8	43.1	55.5	42.6	46.5	44.5	37	35.1	43.7 (8
	0.42	0.45	0.92	0.77	0.62	0.43	0.08	0.12	0.17
	756	11 634	9 139	8 686	10 928	10 672	5 516	10 731	6 409
	387	469	311	386	413	480	169	464	228
	546	570	972	530	482	671	458	496	279
	447	626	528	488	400	506	195	319	271
	3.6	2.2	2.8	2.5	2.7	3.2	3.4	2.8	1.5
	8.4	6.8	7.5	5.8	7.3	7.1	9	5.5	8.2
	3.5	4.5	5.9	8.3	3.8	4.7	16.9	. .	5.3
	2.5	4.8	3.7	5.2	3.2	2.1	16.7	17.2	3.2
	291 [7]	127 658	34 988	26 508	216 157	409 620	8 014	1 589	23 796
	60.1	21.9	26.9	21.9	18.1	25.8	11.4	24.4	54.8
	11.4	7.9	11.1	7.1	11.7	10.6	8.9	8.1	14
	330 [7]	116 729	31 647	26 953	225 260	344 454	19 831	1 655	20 687
	61.1	20	24.3	22.2	18.8	21.7	28.2	25.4	47.6
	12	7.8	7.2	7.2	12.2	15.3	11.9	9	12.4
	541 [7]	12 544	7 445	6 779	25 851	47 729	2 398	307	3 672
	0.9	1.3	2.8	3	1.4	1.7	1.5	2.2	2.1

8.   Included in F
9.   Including no
Sources: Popula
        GDP, GFCF,
        Indicators of
        Wages and p
        Foreign trade
        Total official

	Italy	Japan	Luxembourg	Netherlands	New Zealand	Norway	Portugal
	57 114	123 920	390	15 070	3 406	4 262	9 814
	190	328	150	369	13	13	106
	0.1	0.5	0.6	0.6	0.8	0.4	0
	21 410	63 690	162	6 444	1 451	1 973	4 607
	8.5	6.7	3.7	4.5	10.8	5.9	17.3
	32.3	34.4	31.5	25.5	23.5	23.7	33.9
	59.2	58.9	64.8	69.9	65.7	70.4	48.7
	1 149.9	3 346.4	9.3	289.8	42.2	105.9	68.6
	19 900	27 005	24 186	19 232	12 400	24 853	6 991
	974.6	2 349.2	8.1	248	46.6	71.6	90.1
	16 866	18 957	20 904	16 453	13 675	16 804	9 180
	2.7	4.8	4.3	2.9	−0.2	1.1	4.2
	19.8	31.7	29	20.5	16.4	18.5	26
	9.4	13.1	12.4	10	9.9 (90)	11.7 (87)	7.6
	5.3	5.5	5.5	4.7	4.8 (90)	2.1	4.5 (
	4.1	8.5	9.9	2.5	−1.3	−6.6	8.7
	18.6	35.1	59.4	24.7	15	23.6	25.4
	17.5	9.2	17.1	14.4	16.6	21.5	17.8
′)	49.4	25.4	45 (86)	54.8	..	52.9	39.3 (
′)	43	34.4	52.9 (86)	54.6	..	55.3	37.6 (
	0.29	0.33	0.42	0.87	0.24	1.1	0.31
	10 418	10 738	11 973	9 807	8 771	8 558	5 810
	478	282	470	356 (89)	440	378	260
	555	421	413	462	430	502	263
	423	610	252	485	372	423	176
	1.3	1.6	2.1	2.5	1.9	3.1	2.8
	8.3	4.6	9.2	6.5	8.3	7	10.8
	7.1	4.1	..	2.2	5.2	7.6	..
	5.7	1.9	2.3	1.5	7.2	5.5	11.3
	170 258	286 314	8	131 361	9 515	33 808	16 338
	14.8	8.6	..	45.3	22.5	31.9	23.8
	11.6	8.5	..	10.6	10.5	13.1	17.4
	181 925	233 814	..	126 158	9 464	27 164	24 874
	15.8	7	..	43.5	22.4	25.6	36.3
	12.8	13.1	..	10.9	6.8	4.6	22.6
	44 232	55 179	..	12 289	2 902	10 777	10 182
	2.9	2.8	..	1.2	3.7	4.8	4.9

elgium.
-residential construction.
on and employment: OECD, *Labour Force Statistics.*
and general government: OECD, *National Accounts,* Vol. 1 and *OECD Economic Outlook,* Historical Statistics.
iving standards: miscellaneous national publications.
ces: OECD, *Main Economic Indicators.*
OECD, *Monthly Foreign Trade Statistics,* series A.
eserves: IMF, *International Financial Statistics.*

	Spain	Sweden	Switzerland	Turkey	United Kingdom	United States
	39 025	8 617	6 792	57 693	57 649	252 160
	77	19	165	74	236	27
	0.3	0.3	0.6	2.3	0.2	0.9
	12 608	4 431	3 560	18 171	25 726	116 877
	10.7	3.2	5.5	46.6	2.2	2.9
	33.1	28.2	34.4	20.3	27.8	25.3
	56.3	68.5	60.1	33.1	70	71.8
	527.6	239.3	230.9	108	1 008.4	5 610.8
	13 519	27 774	33 992	1 872	17 492	22 204
	496.2	145.4	148.3	201.1	899.8	5 610.8
	12 714	16 877	21 832	3 486	15 608	22 204
	4.3	1.6	2.2	4.7	2	1.9
	23.9	19.4	25.6	22.8	16.9	15.4
	7.1					
0)	4.7	6.2	16.9⁹	5.8 (87)	3	3.4
	9.9	3.3	4	3.1	2.8	-0.5
	21	16	31.6	21.2	13.5	15
	16.1	27.2	13.9	22.5	21.7	18.2
0)	35.5 (88)	59.8	32.5	..	39.7	36.7
0)	36.3 (88)	60	34.2	..	38.8	32.5
	0.22	0.88	0.37	..	0.32	0.2
	7 935	8 994	12 607	1995	9 912	14 891
	307	418	441	29	361	568
	323	681	905	151	434	509
	389	471	406	174	434	814
	3.9	2.9	3	0.9	1.4	2.3
	7.8	6.1	6.2	56.5	7.4	8.9
	7.6	7.7	..	..	8.6	2.8
	5.9	7.2	3.5	60.3	6.4	4.4
	55 353	57 422	63 893	13 057	184 087	393 812
	10.5	24	27.7	12.1	18.3	7
	17.1	8.1	10.2	12.9	11.5	13.2
	87 449	54 659	69 863	22 566	222 522	494 842
	16.6	22.8	30.3	20.9	22.1	8.8
	21.6	8.8	10	13.5	10.7	6
	36 008	12 644	20 541	4 252	25 201	50 791
	4.9	2.8	3.5	2.3	1.4	1.2

January, 1994

EMPLOYMENT OPPORTUNITIES

Economics Department, OECD

The Economics Department of the OECD offers challenging and rewarding opportunities to economists interested in applied policy analysis in an international environment. The Department's concerns extend across the entire field of economic policy analysis, both macro-economic and micro-economic. Its main task is to provide, for discussion by committees of senior officials from Member countries, documents and papers dealing with current policy concerns. Within this programme of work, three major responsibilities are:

- to prepare regular surveys of the economies of individual Member countries;
- to issue full twice-yearly reviews of the economic situation and prospects of the OECD countries in the context of world economic trends;
- to analyse specific policy issues in a medium-term context for theOECD as a whole, and to a lesser extent for the non-OECD countries.

The documents prepared for these purposes, together with much of the Department's other economic work, appear in published form in the *OECD Economic Outlook, OECD Economic Surveys, OECD Economic Studies* and the Department's *Working Papers* series.

The Department maintains a world econometric model, INTERLINK, which plays an important role in the preparation of the policy analyses and twice-yearly projections. The availability of extensive cross-country data bases and good computer resources facilitates comparative empirical analysis, much of which is incorporated into the model.

The Department is made up of about 75 professional economists from a variety of backgrounds and Member countries. Most projects are carried out by small teams and last from four to eighteen months. Within the Department, ideas and points of view are widely discussed; there is a lively professional interchange, and all professional staff have the opportunity to contribute actively to the programme of work.

Skills the Economics Department is looking for:

a) Solid competence in using the tools of both micro-economic and macro-economic theory to answer policy questions. Experience indicates that this normally requires the equivalent of a PH.D. in economics or substantial relevant professional experience to compensate for a lower degree.

b) Solid knowledge of economic statistics and quantitative methods; this includes how to identify data, estimate structural relationships, apply basic techniques of time series analysis, and test hypotheses. It is essential to be able to interpret results sensibly in an economic policy context.

c) A keen interest in and knowledge of policy issues, economic developments and their political/social contexts.

d) Interest and experience in analysing questions posed by policy-makers and presenting the results to them effectively and judiciously. Thus, work experience in government agencies or policy research institutions is an advantage.

e) The ability to write clearly, effectively, and to the point. The OECD is a bilingual organisation with French and English as the official languages. Candidates must have excellent knowledge of one of these languages, and some knowledge of the other. Knowledge of other languages might also be an advantage for certain posts.

f) For some posts, expertise in a particular area may be important, but a successful candidate is expected to be able to work on a broader range of topics relevant to the work of the Department. Thus, except in rare cases, the Department does not recruit narrow specialists.

g) The Department works on a tight time schedule and strict deadlines. Moreover, much of the work in the Department is carried out in small groups of economists. Thus, the ability to work with other economists from a variety of cultural and professional backgrounds, to supervise junior staff, and to produce work on time is important.

General Information

The salary for recruits depends on educational and professional background. Positions carry a basic salary from FF 262 512 or FF 323 916 for Administrators (economists) and from FF 375 708 for Principal Administrators (senior economists). This may be supplemented by expatriation and/or family allowances, depending on nationality, residence and family situation. Initial appointments are for a fixed term of two to three years.

Vacancies are open to candidates from OECD Member countries. The Organisation seeks to maintain an appropriate balance between female and male staff and among nationals from Member countries.

For further information on employment opportunities in the Economics Department, contact:

Administrative Unit
Economics Department
OECD
2, rue André-Pascal
75775 PARIS CEDEX 16
FRANCE

Applications citing "ECSUR", together with a detailed *curriculum vitae* in English or French, should be sent to the Head of Personnel at the above address.

MAIN SALES OUTLETS OF OECD PUBLICATIONS
PRINCIPAUX POINTS DE VENTE DES PUBLICATIONS DE L'OCDE

ARGENTINA – ARGENTINE
Carlos Hirsch S.R.L.
Galería Güemes, Florida 165, 4° Piso
1333 Buenos Aires   Tel. (1) 331.1787 y 331.2391
Telefax: (1) 331.1787

AUSTRALIA – AUSTRALIE
D.A. Information Services
648 Whitehorse Road, P.O.B 163
Mitcham, Victoria 3132   Tel. (03) 873.4411
Telefax: (03) 873.5679

AUSTRIA – AUTRICHE
Gerold & Co.
Graben 31
Wien I   Tel. (0222) 533.50.14

BELGIUM – BELGIQUE
Jean De Lannoy
Avenue du Roi 202
B-1060 Bruxelles   Tel. (02) 538.51.69/538.08.41
Telefax: (02) 538.08.41

CANADA
Renouf Publishing Company Ltd.
1294 Algoma Road
Ottawa, ON K1B 3W8   Tel. (613) 741.4333
Telefax: (613) 741.5439
Stores:
61 Sparks Street
Ottawa, ON K1P 5R1   Tel. (613) 238.8985
211 Yonge Street
Toronto, ON M5B 1M4   Tel. (416) 363.3171
Telefax: (416)363.59.63

Les Éditions La Liberté Inc.
3020 Chemin Sainte-Foy
Sainte-Foy, PQ G1X 3V6   Tel. (418) 658.3763
Telefax: (418) 658.3763

Federal Publications Inc.
165 University Avenue, Suite 701
Toronto, ON M5H 3B8   Tel. (416) 860.1611
Telefax: (416) 860.1608

Les Publications Fédérales
1185 Université
Montréal, QC H3B 3A7   Tel. (514) 954.1633
Telefax : (514) 954.1635

CHINA – CHINE
China National Publications Import
Export Corporation (CNPIEC)
16 Gongti E. Road, Chaoyang District
P.O. Box 88 or 50
Beijing 100704 PR   Tel. (01) 506.6688
Telefax: (01) 506.3101

DENMARK – DANEMARK
Munksgaard Book and Subscription Service
35, Nørre Søgade, P.O. Box 2148
DK-1016 København K   Tel. (33) 12.85.70
Telefax: (33) 12.93.87

FINLAND – FINLANDE
Akateeminen Kirjakauppa
Keskuskatu 1, P.O. Box 128
00100 Helsinki
Subscription Services/Agence d'abonnements :
P.O. Box 23
00371 Helsinki   Tel. (358 0) 12141
Telefax: (358 0) 121.4450

FRANCE
OECD/OCDE
Mail Orders/Commandes par correspondance:
2, rue André-Pascal
75775 Paris Cedex 16   Tel. (33-1) 45.24.82.00
Telefax: (33-1) 49.10.42.76
Telex: 640048 OCDE

OECD Bookshop/Librairie de l'OCDE :
33, rue Octave-Feuillet
75016 Paris   Tel. (33-1) 45.24.81.67
(33-1) 45.24.81.81
Documentation Française
29, quai Voltaire
75007 Paris   Tel. 40.15.70.00
Gibert Jeune (Droit-Économie)
6, place Saint-Michel
75006 Paris   Tel. 43.25.91.19
Librairie du Commerce International
10, avenue d'Iéna
75016 Paris   Tel. 40.73.34.60
Librairie Dunod
Université Paris-Dauphine
Place du Maréchal de Lattre de Tassigny
75016 Paris   Tel. (1) 44.05.40.13
Librairie Lavoisier
11, rue Lavoisier
75008 Paris   Tel. 42.65.39.95
Librairie L.G.D.J. - Montchrestien
20, rue Soufflot
75005 Paris   Tel. 46.33.89.85
Librairie des Sciences Politiques
30, rue Saint-Guillaume
75007 Paris   Tel. 45.48.36.02
P.U.F.
49, boulevard Saint-Michel
75005 Paris   Tel. 43.25.83.40
Librairie de l'Université
12a, rue Nazareth
13100 Aix-en-Provence   Tel. (16) 42.26.18.08
Documentation Française
165, rue Garibaldi
69003 Lyon   Tel. (16) 78.63.32.23
Librairie Decitre
29, place Bellecour
69002 Lyon   Tel. (16) 72.40.54.54

GERMANY – ALLEMAGNE
OECD Publications and Information Centre
August-Bebel-Allee 6
D-53175 Bonn   Tel. (0228) 959.120
Telefax: (0228) 959.12.17

GREECE – GRÈCE
Librairie Kauffmann
Mavrokordatou 9
106 78 Athens   Tel. (01) 32.55.321
Telefax: (01) 36.33.967

HONG-KONG
Swindon Book Co. Ltd.
13–15 Lock Road
Kowloon, Hong Kong   Tel. 366.80.31
Telefax: 739.49.75

HUNGARY – HONGRIE
Euro Info Service
Margitsziget, Európa Ház
1138 Budapest   Tel. (1) 111.62.16
Telefax : (1) 111.60.61

ICELAND – ISLANDE
Mál Mog Menning
Laugavegi 18, Pósthólf 392
121 Reykjavik   Tel. 162.35.23

INDIA – INDE
Oxford Book and Stationery Co.
Scindia House
New Delhi 110001   Tel.(11) 331.5896/5308
Telefax: (11) 332.5993
17 Park Street
Calcutta 700016   Tel. 240832

INDONESIA – INDONÉSIE
Pdii-Lipi
P.O. Box 269/JKSMG/88
Jakarta 12790   Tel. 583467
Telex: 62 875

IRELAND – IRLANDE
TDC Publishers – Library Suppliers
12 North Frederick Street
Dublin 1   Tel. (01) 874.48.35
Telefax: (01) 874.84.16

ISRAEL
Praedicta
5 Shatner Street
P.O. Box 34030
Jerusalem 91430   Tel. (2) 52.84.90/1/2
Telefax: (2) 52.84.93

ITALY – ITALIE
Libreria Commissionaria Sansoni
Via Duca di Calabria 1/1
50125 Firenze   Tel. (055) 64.54.15
Telefax: (055) 64.12.57
Via Bartolini 29
20155 Milano   Tel. (02) 36.50.83
Editrice e Libreria Herder
Piazza Montecitorio 120
00186 Roma   Tel. 679.46.28
Telefax: 678.47.51
Libreria Hoepli
Via Hoepli 5
20121 Milano   Tel. (02) 86.54.46
Telefax: (02) 805.28.86
Libreria Scientifica
Dott. Lucio de Biasio 'Aeiou'
Via Coronelli, 6
20146 Milano   Tel. (02) 48.95.45.52
Telefax: (02) 48.95.45.48

JAPAN – JAPON
OECD Publications and Information Centre
Landic Akasaka Building
2-3-4 Akasaka, Minato-ku
Tokyo 107   Tel. (81.3) 3586.2016
Telefax: (81.3) 3584.7929

KOREA – CORÉE
Kyobo Book Centre Co. Ltd.
P.O. Box 1658, Kwang Hwa Moon
Seoul   Tel. 730.78.91
Telefax: 735.00.30

MALAYSIA – MALAISIE
Co-operative Bookshop Ltd.
University of Malaya
P.O. Box 1127, Jalan Pantai Baru
59700 Kuala Lumpur
Malaysia   Tel. 756.5000/756.5425
Telefax: 757.3661

MEXICO – MEXIQUE
Revistas y Periodicos Internacionales S.A. de C.V.
Florencia 57 - 1004
Mexico, D.F. 06600   Tel. 207.81.00
Telefax : 208.39.79

NETHERLANDS – PAYS-BAS
SDU Uitgeverij Plantijnstraat
Externe Fondsen
Postbus 20014
2500 EA's-Gravenhage   Tel. (070) 37.89.880
Voor bestellingen: Telefax: (070) 34.75.778

NEW ZEALAND
NOUVELLE-ZÉLANDE
Legislation Services
P.O. Box 12418
Thorndon, Wellington   Tel. (04) 496.5652
Telefax: (04) 496.5698

NORWAY – NORVÈGE
Narvesen Info Center – NIC
Bertrand Narvesens vei 2
P.O. Box 6125 Etterstad
0602 Oslo 6   Tel. (022) 57.33.00
                              Telefax: (022) 68.19.01

PAKISTAN
Mirza Book Agency
65 Shahrah Quaid-E-Azam
Lahore 54000   Tel. (42) 353.601
                              Telefax: (42) 231.730

PHILIPPINE – PHILIPPINES
International Book Center
5th Floor, Filipinas Life Bldg.
Ayala Avenue
Metro Manila   Tel. 81.96.76
                              Telex 23312 RHP PH

PORTUGAL
Livraria Portugal
Rua do Carmo 70-74
Apart. 2681
1200 Lisboa   Tel.: (01) 347.49.82/5
                              Telefax: (01) 347.02.64

SINGAPORE – SINGAPOUR
Gower Asia Pacific Pte Ltd.
Golden Wheel Building
41, Kallang Pudding Road, No. 04-03
Singapore 1334   Tel. 741.5166
                              Telefax: 742.9356

SPAIN – ESPAGNE
Mundi-Prensa Libros S.A.
Castelló 37, Apartado 1223
Madrid 28001   Tel. (91) 431.33.99
                              Telefax: (91) 575.39.98

Libreria Internacional AEDOS
Consejo de Ciento 391
08009 – Barcelona   Tel. (93) 488.30.09
                              Telefax: (93) 487.76.59

Llibreria de la Generalitat
Palau Moja
Rambla dels Estudis, 118
08002 – Barcelona
        (Subscripcions) Tel. (93) 318.80.12
        (Publicacions) Tel. (93) 302.67.23
                              Telefax: (93) 412.18.54

SRI LANKA
Centre for Policy Research
c/o Colombo Agencies Ltd.
No. 300-304, Galle Road
Colombo 3   Tel. (1) 574240, 573551-2
                              Telefax: (1) 575394, 510711

SWEDEN – SUÈDE
Fritzes Information Center
Box 16356
Regeringsgatan 12
106 47 Stockholm   Tel. (08) 690.90.90
                              Telefax: (08) 20.50.21
Subscription Agency/Agence d'abonnements :
Wennergren-Williams Info AB
P.O. Box 1305
171 25 Solna   Tel. (08) 705.97.50
                              Téléfax : (08) 27.00.71

SWITZERLAND – SUISSE
Maditec S.A. (Books and Periodicals - Livres
et périodiques)
Chemin des Palettes 4
Case postale 266
1020 Renens   Tel. (021) 635.08.65
                              Telefax: (021) 635.07.80

Librairie Payot S.A.
4, place Pépinet
CP 3212
1002 Lausanne   Tel. (021) 341.33.48
                              Telefax: (021) 341.33.45

Librairie Unilivres
6, rue de Candolle
1205 Genève   Tel. (022) 320.26.23
                              Telefax: (022) 329.73.18

Subscription Agency/Agence d'abonnements :
Dynapresse Marketing S.A.
38 avenue Vibert
1227 Carouge   Tel.: (022) 308.07.89
                              Telefax : (022) 308.07.99

See also – Voir aussi :
OECD Publications and Information Centre
August-Bebel-Allee 6
D-53175 Bonn (Germany)   Tel. (0228) 959.120
                              Telefax: (0228) 959.12.17

TAIWAN – FORMOSE
Good Faith Worldwide Int'l. Co. Ltd.
9th Floor, No. 118, Sec. 2
Chung Hsiao E. Road
Taipei   Tel. (02) 391.7396/391.7397
                              Telefax: (02) 394.9176

THAILAND – THAÏLANDE
Suksit Siam Co. Ltd.
113, 115 Fuang Nakhon Rd.
Opp. Wat Rajbopith
Bangkok 10200   Tel. (662) 225.9531/2
                              Telefax: (662) 222.5188

TURKEY – TURQUIE
Kültür Yayinlari Is-Türk Ltd. Sti.
Atatürk Bulvari No. 191/Kat 13
Kavaklidere/Ankara   Tel. 428.11.40 Ext. 2458
Dolmabahce Cad. No. 29
Besiktas/Istanbul   Tel. 260.71.88
                              Telex: 43482B

UNITED KINGDOM – ROYAUME-UNI
HMSO
Gen. enquiries   Tel. (071) 873 0011
Postal orders only:
P.O. Box 276, London SW8 5DT
Personal Callers HMSO Bookshop
49 High Holborn, London WC1V 6HB
                              Telefax: (071) 873 8200
Branches at: Belfast, Birmingham, Bristol, Edin-
burgh, Manchester

UNITED STATES – ÉTATS-UNIS
OECD Publications and Information Centre
2001 L Street N.W., Suite 700
Washington, D.C. 20036-4910 Tel. (202) 785.6323
                              Telefax: (202) 785.0350

VENEZUELA
Libreria del Este
Avda F. Miranda 52, Aptdo. 60337
Edificio Galipán
Caracas 106   Tel. 951.1705/951.2307/951.1297
                              Telegram: Libreste Caracas

Subscription to OECD periodicals may also be
placed through main subscription agencies.

Les abonnements aux publications périodiques de
l'OCDE peuvent être souscrits auprès des
principales agences d'abonnement.

Orders and inquiries from countries where Distribu-
tors have not yet been appointed should be sent to:
OECD Publications Service, 2 rue André-Pascal,
75775 Paris Cedex 16, France.

Les commandes provenant de pays où l'OCDE n'a
pas encore désigné de distributeur devraient être
adressées à : OCDE, Service des Publications,
2, rue André-Pascal, 75775 Paris Cedex 16, France.

                                           6-1994

PRINTED IN FRANCE

•

OECD PUBLICATIONS
2 rue André-Pascal
75775 PARIS CEDEX 16
No. 47365
(10 94 13 1) ISBN 92-64-14198-7
ISSN 0376-6438

•